KOSHER
ITALIAN
GOURMET

KOSHER ITALIAN GOURMET

Israel Aharoni   **Shaul Evron**

Photography: **Nelly Schaeffer**
Design: **Sheri Ansky**
English Editor: **Dena Ben-Kiki**
Type set by: **El-Ot Ltd.**
Plates: **Yesh Offset**
Production: **Ruthie Eilat**

Cute, those Italians. The Northerners with the rounded accents, located near the Austrian border, nearly classic Germans, despising the Neapolitan rapscallions no less than the hot blooded Southerners despise them. However, both north and south ascribe the utmost importance to their coffee, their wine, and the food on their plates. 'Espresso' will mean a few droplets of thick and bitter liquid in both regions, and for both, the enemy will be he who overcooked his pasta.

It is a great country, long and divided, impatient, with a cooking history to be proud of. A nation which loves life and knows suffering, one that creates exciting feasts from every-day ingredients. A people that can live with communism or fascism, with the Mafia and with strikes, but will never compromise the olive oil, the tomato, or the red wine.

In this book we attempt to bring the Italian cuisine closer to us, and convey, beyond the recipes, something of the Italian spirit of joy in eating.

About the Book

This book contains eight chapters: Antipasti, Pizzas and Baked Goods, Soups, Pasta, Vegetables, Meat Dishes, Fish, and Desserts.

In order to prepare a classic Italian meal, you should begin with the antipasti – a variety of dishes, or only one – or a dish from the soup or baked goods chapter. Continue with a pasta dish, and then a main dish of poultry, meat, or fish, accompanied by a vegetable, if necessary, and finally – dessert.

At the beginning of the pasta chapter you will find detailed explanations on pasta, fresh and dried, how tos for homemade pasta and cutting, cooking, and filling pasta dough. The amount of pasta per person taken into account for this book, 4 oz., is quite sufficient as a single course for a dinner or as a first course, before a meat dish. The amount may be reduced if antipasti are also to be served.

You can, of course, select a pasta, pizza, or baked recipe, prepare it, and just have fun with it. You can also prepare an excellent pepper salad, and leave it in your refrigerator for a few days.

In the chapter on vegetables you will find many receipes which may be served as complete dishes in their own right, with no need for side dishes. When you prepare a full meal, make sure and plan carefully so as not to overload the cook. At least two dishes should be prepared ahead of time, and only one or two should be assembled during the meal. And don't forget to serve a good wine.

All recipes in this book will serve six, unless otherwise indicated.

Keeping Kosher

All recipes in this book have been adapted to the kosher kitchen. Even so, we felt it would be unauthentic, not to mention phony, to neglect mention of the Italian food as it is – and Italians, do eat milk and meat in the same meal, and enjoy their shellfish. Such ingredients do not appear in the recipes, and we've found excellent replacements for them, but we would not want to belie their existence or 'kosher' the Italians, after all.

About the Photography

When we set out to write an Italian cook book, it was clear that we would do the photography in Italy. We undertook a clear undercurrent throughout the book – color both in format and in content, with Italy underlying and forming a backdrop for the food.

The decision was a daring one, for us: not to photograph in a studio. The photographs were to be set against the background of Italy – and anything

could be construed as background for Italian food: tourist locations, markets, choice locations, an old door, roofs of a small town, a garden, an Italian face – as long as the photographs showed the Italian food at its best, in its natural surroundings, against the colorful Italian background.

Dr. Eli Landau, a friend, chef, and student of things Italian, referred us to Professor Rapetti, head of the Italian Culture Institute in Israel, who referred us to Giorgio Lindo, editor of the Espresso guide – the Italian equivalent of the Michelin. He arranged for us to meet chefs, cooks, and people who deal in food.

Tuscany, one of the most beautiful regions, one of our favorite in Italy, was selected as the photographic arena. The base was in Villa Venezia, about fifteen miles from Florence – an ancient and charming villa, isolated from the world by wooded hills. Much of the food appearing in this book was cooked in its kitchen, and it also supplied some of the charming backgrounds for some of the photographs.

The work was intensive, hard, and fun. We would rise early, and at seven a.m. the whole crew (all six of us) were riding our giant vehicle, equipped with tons of photographic gear and food, on our way to one or another ancient and exquisite site.

There was no lack of surrealistic scenes. We ascended the steep stairs to the highest spot in San Giminiano bearing plates, food, crates, and photography gear – sillier sights have seldom been seen.

The nature of the photography created a situation opposite to the usual one – the studio up and went out. The job of production and styling, which generally included collection of dishes and matching them to the food while using accessories and different backgrounds, became a scouting job. That which took much effort to create in Israel, in the studio, was suddenly everywhere.

"The light in Europe," quoth our photographer, Nelly Schaeffer, "is different and distinctive."

This natural lighting, soft, and often filtered through a layer of clouds, is absorbed by green surfaces and rough stone walls. This is a light which mostly cannot be defined, but it yields qualities so different from the bright contrasting light of Israel – light which precludes any out-of-studio

photography during most hours of the day.
On more than one occasion Nelly made us wait hours until the sun reached its ideal position and when it did – he would urge us to hurry so as not to miss the magic moment. The artificial lighting was meant only to strengthen and support that which was already there.

Before it was united, Italy was divided into states, kingdoms, princedoms, and city-states, each with its own history, culture, and dialect. The effects of neighbors and conquerors was evident in each region in the language, the culture, and the cuisine. In Piemonte (piedmont) there was a French influence, in Lombardy and Ventu there was an Austro-Hungarian effect, in the south, Spanish, and in Sicily – Arabic.
Once it was possible to classify the regions of Italy according to the fat used in cooking: butter in the north, animal fat (cattle) in the center, and olive oil in the south. Nowadays the borders have become less distinct. Risotto is eaten in the south, and the southern pizza has conquered the north.

The joi-de-vivre of the south is founded on a seemingly infinite number of family gatherings and feasts. In spite of the terrible squalor, the Sicilian kitchen is one of the most varied and exotic in all of Italy: Greeks and Romans, Arabs and Spaniards, Turks and Frenchmen – all these have dominated the south, and left their traces in its kitchens. The simple food of the poor may be found here, as well as complex and flamboyant dishes of the ruling aristocracy. The Sicilian kitchen finds a perfect form of expression in such occasions as Mafia weddings.
Olive trees, lemons and oranges, walnuts, pistachios, pine-nuts, almonds, and an enormous number of grapevines cover the fields and lands of Sicily. Sheep, some cattle, and a few goats permitted free pasture produce excellent milk, all of which goes to cheese production.
Sicily is renowned for its preserved fruits and ice-creams. Beyond these, its sea-food dishes are well known, and foremost among these are the fine sardines, tuna, and swordfish. Couscous, cooked in earthenware pots and spiced with saffron, cinnamon, cloves, and nutmeg, is served with a fish preparation flaming with red hot peppers. The residents of Sardinia eat Butregga – mullet or tuna roe, salted and sliced, served in thin wedges with lemon and olive oil; grilled lobster, cooked in boiling water or white wine; octopus in oil, vinegar, garlic, and parsley; giant crabs and shrimps and other sea food cooked in white wine and fresh saffron; stuffed calamary, and jelly-fish cooked in their own ink. All the Mediterranean fish are present in great numbers, fried or grilled, in fish-soup or risotto.
The true Sardinia lies not on the sea-shore but further inland, among the mountains, the forests, the village homes of the farmers and shepherds. It is here that each family manufactures its own olive oil and wine, grows its own vegetables, and prepares its own sausages. Young roasted cattle is the most typical meal. The shepherds still manufacture their own cheese, although industrial manufacture of cheese is not unheard of, and each village has its own characteristic bread.

Vittorio Marketti is a Tuscan nobleman who has lived in Rome for several decades and still feels like an exile. "There are many regions in Italy," he says, "and each has its own style of cooking. The 'Romans' took the best things from each of the regions, and spoiled them." Marketti's statement may be taken with a grain of salt, but it is true that in Rome a mishmash can be found of all Italy's regional cuisines, not always at their best.

When discussing the Lacio region, one refers to Rome and its environs, home to eighty percent of the residents. Although Rome is the capital of Italy and the very heart of the empire, it is not the cooking capital of Italy. The original Rome cuisine is simple, and poor.

In this city, resplendent with castles, renaissance villas, and monuments, a city famous for its feasts and food revelries, a cuisine emerged that is popular, simple, and poor. Few of the recipes used in the castles and Vatican kitchens were preserved, while the cooking of the masses was that which left its mark. Only a few dozen families participated in the Roman banquets, and testimony has survived of such impossible recipes as peacocks and flamingos cooked, complete with their feathers and tails.

The priests and popes loved good food, entertained and were entertained. They ate the prime produce, and the masses had to settle for the second best parts and the leftovers. For this reason the Roman cuisine uses the internal organs, rejected by the nobility and the priesthood, which were dubbed "the fifth quarter".

The principles of Roman cooking are few and simple. A lot of garlic, rosemary, and white wine, sauteed and stewed in olive oil. In this part of central Italy fresh pasta, from the north, meets dried pasta, from the south, and both take star billing. A great deal of internal organs and mutton are eaten there, good Mediterranean sea food, and river fish.

The Romans eat soups, and claim that Julius Caesar's forces went out to conquer the world with their bellies full of whole wheat soup. The vegetables in the Lacio region are excellent, and one of the better known is the Roman artichoke, the 'romanello' or 'romanesque'. This is a soft round artichoke which may be eaten raw. One of the best known of the dishes made of this artichoke is called 'Jewish Artichoke' and was probably taken from the Jewish community in Rome.

Lacio is home to the white Castelli Romani wines, foremost among which is the Frescati. These are dry wines with a slight bouquet of the fruit, and they go well with pasta and sea food. Local red wines are available, as well. The region is given to Sirocco winds, which sometimes damage the vineyards.

The Romans like to eat out, and this tradition started in the taverns, beyond the walls. Wine was sold there, and whole families, old and young, would show up with home cooked food, steaming pots, baked goods, and meats. Wine bottles were sold there, and great sheets of paper for the tables. The families ate, drank, laughed, sang, and fought.

Tuscany

The residents of Tuscany are convinced that the French learned the art of cooking from them. This belief has some foundation, as several of the French Kings married Medici girls, from Florence, and received Italian chefs as part of the dowry. Catherine de Medici, age twelve, brought many chefs and bakers to Henri II's court, as well as much knowledge.

The wedding feast for Catherine de Medici and Henri II was held in Palazzo degli Uffizi, which is a museum today. Twenty four cold dishes were served, eighteen entrees, ten main dishes, fourteen different trays of cheese and fruit, and nine desserts.

Duck a l'orange, omelettes, and pheasants in grapes are of Tuscan origin.

Italian contributions to the French kitchen, which did not necessarily come from Tuscany, are sorbet, ice-cream, fruit preserved in syrup, pasta, and the art of sugar-blowing, which came to being in Venice, inspired by the glass blowing trade.

The Tuscan cooking tradition is related to the rich spiritual life, and to the scientific, political, and artistic ideas born of this region. The Tuscanese brought order and simplicity into cooking. The Tuscan cuisine is simple, but not poor. The food is natural, not covered with sauces, and based on wine, olive oil, and fresh spices, primarily sage, basil, and rosemary. The most common cooking techniques are charcoal grilling with aromatic chestnut wood, and frying in olive oil.

The characteristic cheeses in the Tuscany region are pecurino and marzolino. There are wonderful mushrooms here: porcini, pronuli, and truffles. Chestnut trees grow wild, and chestnuts themselves star in many dishes. A poor-man's dish, a kind of polente, was prepared of chestnut flour, and the wood was used for charcoal grilling.

One of the prime ingredients in this region is the olive oil. It is light, delicate, and not as dark as the southern oil. It's color is golden, or light green.

Tuscan has a long lasting enmity with the Piemonte region, for first place in red wines – an enmity reminiscent of that between Bordeaux and Burgandy, in France. The best known local wines are the Brunello de-Montelcino and the Cianti.

One of the heights of the Tuscan cuisine is the Bistecca Fiorentina. This is a T-bone cut weighing about two pounds, from a calf aged between veal and grown cattle. This steak is roasted on a grill, and the residents of Florence may be divided into those who salt, pepper, and olive-oil their bistecca before the roasting, and those who do so after roasting.

Liguria

This is the Italian riviera region, located in the north-west, just outside the actual boot – a long and narrow strip of beach, surrounded by mountains. What is amazing is that, in spite of the fact that it is a coastal region, no great use is made of fish and sea food, probably because the men here dealt in sailing, not fishing.

For this reason, the residents developed food which kept for a long time and 'travelled well' – different dried grains, dry sausages, preserves, and dry baked goods. Another result was that the men, who spent most of their sailing time existing off their dried and preserved food, lovingly stored their fresh vegetables and herbs grown in and preserved in this region. Liguria is renowned for its wonderful variety of herbs, and almost all its dishes are made green by them. Particularly famous is the Pesto sauce, which is based on the specially aromatic basil, which lends its taste to pastas, vegetable dishes, and many others.

The Liguria region borders on French Provence, and both regions have a lot in common, on the culinary level.

The fishing here is poor, consisting mainly of sardine and anchovy, which were preserved for the above mentioned reasons. Red meat is seldom used here, of course, and veal and chicken take its place.

Piemonte (Piedmont)

The Piemonte region – at the foot of the mountain, a kind of Italian refuge within France, or perhaps a French refuge within Italy, is one of the strongholds of Italian cuisine. This was once a part of the French Savoy region. The official language was French, as was the cooking. In 1797 a book was published in Turin, the regional capital. It was a cookbook, named "Pimontese Cooking – Parisian Perfection". Therefore the Pimontese cuisine is a combination of the French and Italian, and it enjoys the best of both worlds – butter and olive oil.

In the mountain rivers of Piemonte one may find trout and wonderful fresh-water fish. This is the largest cattle-raising region in Italy, and excels in cattle and in butter and cheese. In the autumn there are pheasants and grouse, wild ducks and other game. This is also the grape-gathering season in the vineyards, and the frog, snail, and forest-mushroom season.

This region is known for truffles – white mushrooms. In season these appear in almost every dish, and their aroma is prominent throughout the land. These are grated, on a special instrument, over pastas and other cooked dishes, just before serving. Unlike the French, who find the black truffles aided by trained pigs, the Italians gather theirs with trusty trained dogs.

Turin, capital of the Piemonte region, is an elegant Baroque city on the banks of the river Po. In the 18th century a cocoa industry was established here, through which chocolate made its way into Europe. Turin also contributed the greasing – thin crispy bread sticks, pre meal munchies. Generally Turin is famous for wonderful baked goods and wonderful cafes. The most characteristic cheese is the fontina. It is prepared in the Osta valley of cow's milk, in giant crocks each weighing forty pounds. Fontina cheese made of summer milk is better and more expensive than winter milk cheese, since the cows graze in summer, and their milk is richer and more aromatic. Goats cheese, such as rubiola, is also prepared in this region. Piemonte is one of Italy's most prominent wine regions. It excels in its strong red wines, most famous of which are the barolo and the barbosa.

During the 'New Wine Festival' a kind of hot sauce is cooked on a small tabletop range where peppers, celery, artichoke, cauliflower, Jerusalem artichoke, and many more vegetables are dipped. On 'All Saints Eve' minestrone soup is eaten with peas, smoked meats, sage, and rosemary.

Lombardy

Lombardy is one of the most varied regions in Italy. Geographically it is a checkerboard of planes and valleys, wooded hills, lakes, and mountains. The classic cooking here is a concatenation of traditions. The cooking of nobility, poor, popular cooking, and the effects of neighbors and conquerors: the Spaniards passed by and left their mark, and the effects of the Austro-Hungarian reign can be perceived to this very day. The towns of Lombardy differ in their cooking traditions, despite their physical proximity. Bergamo is more Venetian the Lombardian, and Mantua is reminiscent of southern Emilia. But there are several things in common: butter, cream, risotto, and polenta.

Rice was originally the domain of rich city folk, and to this day it is served at weddings, and on Sunday dinners. Almost every ingredient on hand is put into the rice – vegetables, fish, and meat. The best known rice dishes are the saffroned Risotto Milenese, and the Risotto Cartozina, made with sea-food.

The other characteristic dish is polenta, a sort of porridge made of corn meal, which came originally from Venice, but is now a local favorite. It is prepared in dozens of different variations: with water and with milk, mixed with other cereals, or with butter and cheese, with tomatoes, lard, vegetables, and sausages. Polenta may be served warm and thick, or cooled. sliced, and fried.

Lombardy is a cattle raising region, and it supplies the greater part of Italy's dairy production. Many cheeses are prepared here, local specialties and others: mascrapone, rubiola, belpaese, Gorgonzola, and garna-padne.
The dried meats are prominent in Lombardy's antipasto: the sausages, Millanese salami, mortadella, and frankfurters.

Veneto

Venice, capital of Veneto, has been a sea farers' city for many generations, and sent ships to all seven seas, but especially to the Far East. The Venetians brought rice and exotic spices to Italy, and to this day rice is a star in Venice cuisine. Risotto is served in many forms – with vegetables, sea food, and meat. One of the best known Veneto foods is a black risotto, which gets its color from the squids' ink. Another holiday dish is called Risi A-Bisi – rice with peas.
The proximity of the sea makes the Veneto region wealthy in fish and sea food, cooked and served in every possible manner. Almost all cuts and kinds of meat are served in Veneto, as well as internal organs. A classic Venetian dish is liver fried in onions. Game, ducks, rabbits, and game birds can also be found here.
The characteristic Veneto wines are white and light – pinot grigir (grey), and chardonnay.

Herbs and Spices

You cannot discuss Italian food without mentioning herbs. All herbs may be purchased dry, in which form they can be used, but fresh herbs are better. Many specialty stores carry fresh herbs. Buy them as they are and arrange them in a glass of water, like flowers, then refrigerate.
An even better way to ascertain a supply of fresh herbs is to pay a visit to a nearby plant nursery, spend a few cents on herbs, and plant them in flowerpots. You need not be an expert gardener for this, just water occasionally, and you will have a good supply of herbs.
Here are some of the main herbs you should keep handy: Sage, rosemary, oregano, marjoram, thyme, and basil. It is worth that little effort. The herbs will spice and enrich the food you cook.

Olive Oil

Olive oil is an important ingredient in Italian cuisine, and massive quantities of it are used both for cooking and for seasoning. The Italians have a great variety of olive oils, marvelously gentle, virgin oils, young ones, clear and fresh or thick, dark, and almost coarse.
Each region has its own oil, each dish calls for its own variety of oil.
Make sure that the olive oil you purchase is of the finest quality available, cold pressed, and more than anything else – be sure to use enough oil.

Cheeses

Mozzarella – mostly comes in balls, this is a soft white cheese, excellent for pizzas.
Riccotta – a white cheese, very soft, should be as fresh a possible, and used for desserts and filling various pastas.
Parmesan – a hard and spicy cheese. It is used in small quantities, on account of its strong flavor, over pastas, on fillings, and for many other dishes.

Antipasti are not anti-pasta fighters, but rather the appetizers, prelude to the meal itself. 'Ante' means before, in Latin, and pasti (singular, pasto) means food. Do not confuse these with pasta, which means dough.

Antipasti: long tables, laden with dozens of dishes, a wealth of smells and colors. Homemade sausages and home cured meats; fresh sheep cheese floating in olive oil, fried cheeses and sharp dry cheeses; vegetables raw, pickled, cooked, and steamed, warm and cold, hot, spiced lightly, or floating in a rich sauce; shellfish of all kinds, prepared in every conceivable manner. One must constantly remind oneself not to overindulge. The antipasti are followed by pasta, a main course, and finally, a dessert. But this wisdom is hard to follow when one is faced with a wide and tempting variety of antipasti. The types found on the banquet table vary regionally. On the coast the emphasis is on fresh fish, clams, sea urchins, lobsters, and a variety of shrimps – but these will not be found on every table.

In Folia, on the shores of the Adriatic sea, in the heel section of the Italian 'boot', evenings are spent in the huge seaside restaurants. Each of these a large seawater pool, wherein rest neatly stacked crates of seafood. The diner selects a fish or crab that meets his fancy, and a hefty Italian, armed with a knife, prepares the antipasti. He will crack the clams, chop the tiny squid and the sea urchins. A drop of lemon juice, and the contented diner can wait for the pasta or main course, in delicious appreciation of the antipasti.

Clams, calamary, and squid – in the south these will be cooked with tomatoes, further north vinegar will be used, but always with olive oil. Tiny fish, fetched by the fishermen of morning, will be piled on the table, lightly fried, marinated, or salted.

Ever since Columbus, Genoa and its environs have always been home to bold seafarers, not fishermen. The regional specialty is preserved fish, that a seaman could take along on a lengthy voyage. You will find anchovy fish, which made the trip from Spain in wooden casks, and canned Portuguese sardines, on every antipasti table. These are served as they come, in fish or meat sauces, or cooked with vegetables.

The farther inland one travels, the more one finds vegetables on the antipasti table. Tomatoes prepared in endless variety: fresh, sliced and served with mozzarella, olive oil, and basil; sun-dried, salted, pickled, and baked. Each tomato is selected, as in a boutique, because the Italians remember the secret we tend to forget: before you begin to spice and cook, the tomato must be a good tomato.

Each vegetable has its own manner of preparation. Artichoke hearts, tiny zucchini, peppers of all colors and flavors, fresh green beans, dried kidney beans, broad or narrow, short or long green beans. Mushrooms grow wild in a great wealth, variety, vitality, and they are served raw, steamed, and fried. And olives... there is not another nation which is so pedantic about its olives: their breed, their picking, and their processing. In the south olives are picked when they are very ripe, and then they and their oil have a rich and heavy flavor; in Tuscany they are picked much earlier, and the olives and oils have a young, pristine flavor. Most antipasti dishes receive a shade of flavor, be it strong or mild, from the use of olives and olive oil, and their combination with herbs.

Sausages and cold cuts are given top billing in the antipasti. These are prepared differently in each region. There are the finely ground Millanese salami and the more coarsely prepared Tuscanese salami; the hot Southern frankfurters, and a wide variety of salt cured beef, ranging from the noble Parma all the way to the crudely homemade peasant variety. This is generally served with melon, figs, or fresh mozzarella.

The sausage antipasti will vary in taste not only from region to region, but even from farm to farm, or from restaurant to restaurant, since each cook prepares his sausages and cold cuts in the time honored way taught by his father and grandfather. These meats are not usually accompanied by vegetables, fish, or cheese. They are placed on a board or plate, mostly without bread, always without butter.

Leftovers play an important role in the making of antipasti. Yesterday's bread turns into moist bread salad with chopped vegetables, olive oil, and herb seasoning. This same bread may take a moment in the oven, and return under a mound of cold tomatoes and olive oil (bruschetta), or a rich spread made of internal organs (crostini).

CROSTINI WITH GOAT CHEESE AND TOMATOES

crostini alla napoletana

These are lightly toasted slices of French bread, covered with a thick spread. Two or three different varieties can be offered at the same time.

INGREDIENTS:

12 slices French bread, 1 inch thick
A little olive oil
12 slices goat cheese
12 slices tomatoes
Salt and freshly ground black
  pepper
1 tablespoon finely chopped basil
  leaves

1. Dribble a little olive oil on each slice of bread and toast under a grill until golden.

2. Place a slice of cheese on each slice of bread, and cover with a slice of tomato.

3. Dribble some more olive oil, and season with salt and pepper. Sprinkle some chopped basil on tomato slices.

4. Place under the broiler for 2-3 minutes and serve at once.

CROSTINI WITH WHITE BEANS SPREAD

crostini con fagioli

INGREDIENTS:

1 cup dried white beans
2 tablespoons quality olive oil
1 oz. softened butter
1 chopped garlic clove
1 tablespoon rosemary
3/4 cup stock or water
Salt and freshly ground black
  pepper
Juice of 1 lemon
12 slices French bread, 1 inch thick
A little olive oil

1. Soak beans overnight in plenty of cold water.

2. Drain, put in a saucepan with 4 cups of water and 1 teaspoon salt and bring to a boil. Reduce heat and cook, covered, for 1 1/2 hours, or until beans are very tender. Drain and allow to cool.

3. Put beans in a food-processor fitted with a steel blade and work to a smooth puree.

4. Heat olive oil and butter in a large frying pan. Add garlic and rosemary, fry for 1 minute, add bean puree and combine thorouhly.

5. Gradually add stock or water, stirring constantly, until mixture is uniform. Season with salt and pepper and cook a further 10 minutes. Stir in lemon juice.

6. Dribble a little olive oil on bread and toast until golden.

7. Generously spread toasted bread with pureed beans – hot or cold – and serve.

CROSTINI WITH OLIVE AND ANCHOVY SPREAD

crostini con olivi e acciughe

INGREDIENTS:

3 oz. pitted olives
6 anchovy fillets
1 1/2 oz. pine nuts
2 oz. finely grated Parmesan
Freshly ground black pepper
1/4 cup olive oil
12 slices French bread, 3/4 inch
  thick
Olive oil

1. Put olives, anchovies, pine nuts and Parmesan in a food-processor fitted with a steel blade, and work to a smooth puree. Season with pepper and gradually add olive oil.

2. Dribble a little olive oil on bread. Spread a generous layer of olive mixture and toast under a broiler for 1-2 minutes.

OLIVE CROSTINI

INGREDIENTS:

1/4 cup olive oil
1 chopped garlic clove
12 coarsely chopped mushrooms
  (champignon or others)
3 oz. black olives, pitted and
  coarsely chopped
Salt and freshly ground black
  pepper
12 slices French bread, 3/4 inch
  thick
Olive oil

1. Heat oil in a frying pan, add garlic and fry for 1 minute. Add chopped mushrooms and stir-fry for 2-3 minutes. Add olives, season with salt and pepper, stir, and transfer to a bowl.

2. Dribble a little olive oil on bread and toast under a broiler until golden.

3. Spread with a generous layer of olive spread.

CROSTINI WITH LIVER SPREAD

crostini alla toscana

INGREDIENTS:

A little olive oil
10 chicken livers
1 chopped garlic clove
4 chopped fresh sage leaves, or 1
*   teaspoon dried sage*
2 tablespoons chopped capers
⅓ cup dry red wine
Salt and freshly ground black
*   pepper*
12 slices French bread, ¾ inch
*   thick*
Olive oil

1. Heat oil in a large frying pan. When very hot, add livers and fry for 2-3 minutes on both sides. Remove from pan, allow to cool and chop.

2. Fry garlic and sage for about 2 minutes in the same pan. Add capers and stir. Add chopped livers and wine, season with salt and pepper, and cook for 10 minutes.

3. Dribble a little olive oil on bread and toast until golden.

4. Spread toasted bread with a generous layer of liver mixture. Serve either hot or cold.

VARIATION: Add 3 chopped anchovy fillets at step 2.

A variety of fresh vegetables
in an Italian market.

CROSTINI WITH SPLEEN*

Crostini di milza

INGREDIENTS:

1 lb. calf spleen
1/3 cup olive oil
1 finely chopped garlic clove
1 finely chopped onion
3 tablespoons finely chopped
   parsley
1 cup dry red wine
6 chopped anchovy fillets
2 tablespoons chopped capers
Salt and freshly ground black
   pepper
12 slices French bread, 3/4 inch
   thick
Olive oil

1. Remove skin from spleen and chop.

2. Heat olive oil in a large frying pan. Add the garlic and onion and fry until soft.

3. Add chopped spleen and parsley and fry for about 10 minutes, stirring often.

4. Add wine and anchovies, season with salt and pepper and add capers. Reduce heat and cook for 45 minutes.

5. Dribble a little olive oil on each slice of bread and toast under a broiler for a few minutes, until golden.

6. Spread the toasted bread with a generous layer of spleen mixture and serve.

* This spread will keep in the fridge for a week, if chilled.

BRUSCHETTA

INGREDIENTS:

6 slices coarse peasant bread
2 crushed garlic cloves
1/4 cup olive oil
6 ripe tomatoes
Salt and freshly ground black
   pepper

1. Cut each slice of bread in half, sprinkle with olive oil and spread with crushed garlic.

2. Blanch tomatoes in boiling water, peel and dice.

3. Toast bread for a few minutes under a hot broiler, until lightly browned.

4. Arrange slices on a large serving dish. Pile each slice with 1-2 tablespoons chopped tomatoes, season with salt and pepper and sprinkle with a little olive oil.

VARIATION: Add a small, finely chopped onion and 3 anchovy fillets to the tomatoes. Mix well, spread on bread and serve.

A delicious way to use leftovers: yesterday's bread, slightly overripe tomatoes, cooked and flavored spleen. Garlic, basil and olive oil turn the bruschetta and crostini into a marvelous opening to a Tuscan meal.

RAW MUSHROOM SALAD

insalata di funghi

INGREDIENTS:

10 oz. fresh, firm button
    mushrooms
1/2 cup olive oil
Juice of 1 lemon
1 chopped garlic clove
2 tablespoons chopped parsley
Salt and freshly ground black
    pepper

1. Rinse mushrooms, then wipe
dry.

2. Thinly slice mushrooms and
place in a serving bowl.

3. Mix olive oil, lemon juice, garlic,
and parsley in a separate bowl, and
season with salt and pepper. Pour
dressing over mushrooms, mix and
serve.

BREAD SALAD

panzanella

INGREDIENTS:

10 slices Italian-style white bread,
    at least 3 days old
2 ripe tomatoes, blanched, peeled,
    seeded and chopped
1 small onion, chopped
1 sweet red pepper, seeded and
    finely diced
1 green pepper, seeded and finely
    diced
6 small radishes, diced
20-30 finely chopped basil leaves
3 tablespoons finely chopped
    parsley
salt and freshly ground black
    pepper
1/4 cup olive oil
1/2 tablespoon wine vinegar

1. Remove crust from slices of
bread. Soak slices in cold water for
about 15 minutes.

2. Squeeze bread to remove as
much moisture as possible, and
crumble into a large serving bowl.

3. Add chopped vegetables, basil,
and parsley, season with salt and
pepper, and mix well. Add olive oil
and vinegar, mix and serve.

GREEN ALMOND SALAD

insalata di mandrole verde

Green almonds, or almond pods before they dry, are only available one month in the year, in early summer. They are marvelous and delicate, and make delicious dishes. Before buying, bite one almond to make sure the inner shell has not hardened and the kernel is still soft.

INGREDIENTS:

1 lb. green almonds
1/4 cup olive oil
Juice of 1 lemon
2 tablespoons finely chopped dill
Salt and freshly ground black
 pepper

1. Wash almonds thoroughly. Crack shells with a wooden mallet.

2. Bring a large pan of salted water to the boil. Add almonds and cook for 6-7 minutes. Or, steam for 8-10 minutes. Drain and transfer to a bowl.

3. Add remaining ingredients, stir and allow to rest for an hour. Serve at room temperature.

ZUCCHINI SALAD

insalata di zucchini

INGREDIENTS:

6 fresh, young zucchini
Oil for deep frying
1/4 cup quality olive oil
1/4 cup wine vinegar
2 chopped garlic cloves
salt and freshly ground black
 pepper
1 tablespoon chopped mint leaves

1. Slice the ends from the zucchini, cut in half lengthwise, then cut each half into 3 equal-sized pieces.

2. Deep-fry the zucchini for about 3 minutes. Remove with a slotted spoon to paper towels and allow to cool.

3. Put the zucchini in a large serving bowl and season with salt and pepper. Add olive oil, vinegar and mint and mix well. Cover with tinfoil and chill for at least 2 hours before serving.

EGGPLANT AND MOZZARELLA FRIES

INGREDIENTS:

2 medium, firm eggplants
2 teaspoons salt
1 ball fresh mozzarella
A handful of fresh basil leaves

BATTER:

2 eggs
1 cup flour
Freshly ground black pepper
Oil for deep frying

1. Cut each eggplant in half, lengthwise. Cut each half into 3/4 inch thick slices. Cut each slice in half crosswise, almost to the bottom, but leave the two slices attached. Sprinkle with salt, and set aside for 1 hour.

2. Rinse the eggplants thoroughly and dry on paper toweling.

3. Cut the mozzarella into 1/2 inch slices. Season lightly with salt and pepper. Put a slice of mozzarella and a basil leaf between each two attached eggplant slices.

4. To make the batter, put flour in a bowl, add eggs, and beat. Add enough water for a cream-like consistency, beating all the time.

5. Heat oil for deep frying. Dip each eggplant sandwich in the batter and deep-fry until golden. Drain on paper toweling and serve.

ARTICHOKES IN AN OLIVE OIL AND LEMON DRESSING

carciofi con olio e limone

INGREDIENTS:

12 small artichokes
1 lemon
½ cup olive oil
Juice of 1 lemon
2 tablespoons parsley
Salt and freshly ground black
    pepper

1. Slice off and discard the top two-thirds of artichokes. Rub surface of bottom third with half a lemon to prevent discoloration. Clean and trim the stem to within 4 inches of base. Remove tough outer leaves and leave only a few of the inner leaves. Remove chokes from artichoke hearts and rub the insides immediately with a little lemon juice.

2. Fill a large pan with slightly salted water, bring to a boil and cook the artichokes for about 15 minutes. Drain and rinse.

3. Place the cooked artichokes, cut side down, in a deep serving dish.

4. Mix olive oil, lemon juice and parsley in a separate bowl. Season with salt and pepper and stir. Pour dressing over artichokes, allow to rest for an hour and serve at room temperature.

MARINATED SARDINES

INGREDIENTS:

24 fresh sardines, filleted and
    rinsed
½ cup olive oil
½ cup wine vinegar
2 finely chopped scallion roots
1 tablespoon thyme
Salt and freshly ground black
    pepper

1. Heat the olive oil in a frying pan and fry the sardines for 1-2 minutes on each side. Remove from pan with a slotted spoon and place in a wide dish.

2. In a small saucepan, place vinegar, onion, thyme, salt and pepper to taste. Bring to a boil. Pour boiling marinade over sardines, cover and chill for at least 24 hours.

VARIATION: While frying sardines, add 2-3 chopped garlic cloves and 1 chopped hot chilli.

PEPERONATA

INGREDIENTS:

2 sweet red peppers
2 yellow peppers
2 green peppers
$\frac{1}{2}$ cup quality olive oil
2 tablespoons wine vinegar
Salt and freshly ground black
 pepper

1. Halve peppers lengthwise, remove seeds, rinse, and dry.

2. Brush the peppers with olive oil inside and out and broil, skin side up, for about 15 minutes.

3. Place broiled peppers in a plastic bag while still hot, and close bag. Allow to "sweat" for about 10 minutes, to ease peeling. Remove from bag and peel off the skins.

4. Cut peppers into 1 inch cubes, place in a large dish and add olive oil and vinegar. Season with salt and pepper to taste, mix well, cover, and chill for at least 2 hours.

PEPPER, ANCHOVY, AND CAPERS SALAD

insalata di peperoni, acciuga e capperi

INGREDIENTS:

2 sweet red peppers
2 yellow peppers
$\frac{1}{2}$ cup quality olive oil
4 chopped anchovy fillets
2 tablespoons coarsely chopped
 capers
1 tablespoon finely chopped basil
 leaves
1 chopped garlic clove
Salt and freshly ground black
 pepper

1. Preheat oven to medium-high (400 F., 200 C.). Cut the peppers lengthwise, remove seeds, rub with olive oil inside and out, and bake in preheated oven for about 20 minutes.

2. Place baked peppers in a plastic bag while still hot and close bag. Allow to "sweat" for about 10 minutes, to ease peeling. Remove from bag and peel skins. Cut into long, 1 inch wide strips, and place in a flat serving dish.

3. Mix oil, anchovies, capers, basil leaves, and garlic. Season with salt and pepper to taste and pour over peppers. Cover and chill for several hours.

ORANGE, ONION AND FENNEL SALAD

insalata di arancia, cipolla e finocchio

INGREDIENTS:

3 oranges
1 medium onion
3 scallions
2 small fennel bulbs
1 chopped garlic clove
Salt and freshly ground black
    pepper
½ cup olive oil
1 tablespoon wine vinegar

1. Peel the oranges and remove white pith. Halve each orange lengthwise, and slice each half across into ½ inch slices.

2. Peel onion, halve lengthwise, and slice each half finely. Slice the scallions into 1½ inch pieces.

3. Remove the tough outer leaves of the fennel bulbs and slice thinly, lengthwise.

4. Place orange slices, onions and fennel in a salad bowl. Add garlic, season with salt and pepper, pour over the olive oil and vinegar, and mix well. Allow to rest for 20 minutes at room temperature and serve.

TRIPE SALAD

insalata di tripa

INGREDIENTS:

1¼ *lb. tripe*
4 tablespoons vinegar
¾ *cup olive oil*
Juice of 1 lemon
1 small onion, chopped
1 small carrot, diced
3 tablespons chopped parsley
1 tablespoon chopped basil leaves
1 chopped garlic clove
Salt and freshly ground black
*   pepper*

1. Thoroughly clean tripe under running water. Place in a large bowl, add water and 2 tablespons vinegar. Soak for 2 hours. Rinse well.

2. Boil a large saucepan of water with 1 teaspoon salt and 2 tablespoons vinegar. Add tripe and cook over a low heat for 2 hours. Remove, drain and rinse.

3. Cut tripe into long, narrow strips some ½ inch wide. Place in a salad bowl, add remaining ingredients, and mix well. Allow to rest for 2 hours before serving.

Rosina threading hot peppers to dry in the Florence marketplace. Rosina is the oldest stall-owner in the market, and Fabio, much younger than her, owns the "Cibreo" restaurant near the market. His cooking lends a Nouvelle Cuisine delicacy to simple, traditional Tuscan dishes.

MOZZARELLA AND TOMATOES

pomodori e mozzarella

INGREDIENTS:

6 ripe tomatoes
1/2 lb. mozzarella cheese
6 tablespoons virgin oil
2 tablespoons wine vinegar
Salt and freshly ground black
    pepper
2 tablespoons coarsely chopped
    basil leaves

1. Slice tomatoes across into
1/4 inch slices.

2. Slice the mozzarella into 1/4 inch
slices.

3. In a large flat dish, arrange the
tomato and cheese slices
intermittently, slightly overlapping.

4. Dribble the olive oil and vinegar
over the tomatoes and cheese, and
season with salt and pepper to
taste. Sprinkle basil on top and
serve.

STUFFED TOMATOES

pomodori ripieni

INGREDIENTS:

12 large, firm plum tomatoes
1 cup chopped parsley
4-8 chopped garlic cloves
³/₄ cup quality olive oil
Salt and freshly ground black
*   pepper*

1. Preheat oven to medium (350° F., 180° C.).

2. Halve tomatoes lengthwise. Using a teaspoon, hollow out the flesh to make 24 "bowls".

3. Mix parsley, garlic, oil and season with salt and pepper to taste.

4. Fill tomato halves with the parsley mixture.

5. Place the tomatoes in an oven-proof dish, and bake for about 45 minutes. Sprinkle with olive oil every once in a while during baking.
Serve at room temperature.

The tomatoes were picked the day before, the parsley is fresh and crisp. The shorter the way from the market to the oven, the tastier the dish.

EGGPLANT SALAD

insalata di melanzane

INGREDIENTS:

3 small, firm eggplants
1 tablespoon salt
Oil for deep frying
1/2 cup olive oil
2 finely chopped garlic cloves
4 chopped anchovy fillets
1/4 cup wine vinegar
4 tablespoons finely chopped
  parsley
Salt and freshly ground black
  pepper

1. Peel eggplants and cut into
1 inch cubes. Place in one layer on
a tray, and sprinkle with salt. Allow
to rest for 30 minutes, rinse well
under running water, and dry
thoroughly.

2. Heat the oil for deep frying. Fry
the eggplant cubes, several at a
time, until nicely browned. Remove
with a slotted spoon, drain well and
pat with paper towels to remove
excess oil.

3. Heat the olive oil in a saucepan.
Add the garlic and anchovies and
fry gently. Add vinegar and parsley
and cook for about 2 minutes.

4. Place the fried eggplants in a
bowl, pour the hot dressing on top,
season with salt and pepper to
taste and mix well. Serve either hot
or at room temperature.

BEAN SALAD

insalata di fagioli

INGREDIENTS:

2 cups dried white beans
1 carrot, sliced into 1 inch pieces
1 onion, quartered
2 celery stalks, sliced into 1 inch
  pieces
10 fresh sage leaves, or
  1 teaspoon dried sage
1 sprig fresh rosemary, or
  1 teaspoon dried rosemary
1/2 cup quality olive oil
Juice of 1 lemon
1 small onion, finely chopped
2 tablespoons finely chopped
  parsley
2 chopped garlic cloves
Salt and freshly ground black
  pepper

1. Soak the beans overnight in
plenty of water. Drain and rinse.

2. Place the beans in saucepan and
add 2 quarts water, the carrot,
onion, celery, sage and rosemary.
Bring to a boil, reduce flame and
cook until beans are tender but not
mushy (about 1 hour).

3. Drain beans and discard as
much of the vegetables and herbs
as possible. Transfer to a large
bowl.

4. Add the olive oil, lemon juice,
parsley and garlic. Season with salt
and pepper to taste, mix and allow
to rest, covered, for at least an
hour.

EGGPLANTS WITH MOZZARELLA AND TOMATOES

melanzane con mozzarella e pomodori

INGREDIENTS:

2 small, narrow eggplants
3 tablespoons olive oil
3 mozzarella balls
3 ripe, thinly sliced tomatoes
Salt and freshly ground black
  pepper
1 tablespoon chopped basil leaves

1. Slice eggplants across into
1/2 inch slices. Place in a single
layer on a tray, sprinkle with salt
and set aside for 30 minutes. Rinse
well and dry thoroughly.

2. Brush the eggplants with olive
oil. Broil for a few minutes, until
browned.

3. Leaving the eggplant on the
same broiling pan, place a slice of
cheese and a tomato slice on each
slice of egplant. Sprinkle with a
little olive oil, season with salt and
pepper and garnish with basil.
Return to grill and broil a further
2-3 minutes. Serve immediately.

Put commercial pizzas out of your mind. The ones with raglike, moistened dough, covered with canned tomato puree, and a pile of cheap yellow cheese. This is not pizza. Fresh tomatoes, garlic, a little basil and olive oil, over properly made dough – these will make all the difference.

The pizza may be the best known Italian baked product. The idea is simple, and simply wonderful. A simple dough base, with crispy brown edges that snap at the bite, and a softer center, bearing a variety of flavors. All this spends a while in the oven, and the result tastes good, is pleasant and pretty. At its best, this can be truly excellent.

The possibilities presented by pizza are infinite: vegetables, sausages, mushrooms, cheese, olive oil, seasoning. There are open faced pizzas, and closed ones, where the dough is folded round the filling. The original theme makes way for variations, and you need be concerned only the quality of your groceries.

The best cheese for pizzas is the mozzarella. It is very delicate, delicious, and melts well when baked. Parmesan is also very good for pizza, but it must not be overdone, as it is very strong.

The Italian pizza parlours are very pleasant places. The tables are made of wood and the atmosphere is neighborly. In the center of the parlor an oven contains the eternal flame. Nimble bakers poke long wooden utensils into the oven, with edges burnt with constant use. The pizzas go in and out at a staggering pace. They are baked on the spot, not prepared and then reheated. Piping hot, the pizzas are borne well above the waiters' heads, and served with simple red wine.

Pizzas are not the Italian's only baked specialty. There are many kinds of bread: peasant bread, white or black, risen or flat. There is the bland saltless Tuscany bread, eaten with rich spicy stews and taking on their flavors.

Focaccia is a flat and very simple bread – reminiscent of Israeli pocket bread. Before the baking, dimples are made in the bread with one finger, and filled with a liberal serving of olive oil and coarse (kosher) salt. This is simple and delicious home bread, which fills the house with dizzying baking aroma. Fried onion and rosemary may be added at the last minute. This is eaten very fresh, as soon as possible after it leaves the oven. Another department is that of the more complicated baked goods: salty crisp tarts, with richly varied fillings. Cheeses, eggs, mushrooms, and different vegetables. These are more festive bakes, which can be part of a simple meal.

FLATBREAD WITH OLIVE OIL

focaccia

INGREDIENTS:

1 oz. yeast
1 lb. flour
1/3 cup quality olive oil
1/2 tablespoon coarse salt

1. Dissolve the yeast in 1/4 cup lukewarm water. Add enough flour to make a very soft dough. Cover and let rise for about 30 minutes in a warm place.

2. Place remaining flour in a large bowl, make a large well in the center. Slowly pour in 3/4 cup lukewarm water. Add the yeast mixture and mix well. If dough is too sticky, add a little flour.

3. Place dough on a lightly floured working surface. Knead well for about 5 minutes. Shape into a ball, place in a warm bowl, cover with a damp towel, and allow to rise in a warm place for about 30 minutes.

4. Knead dough again for several minutes. Roll out to a square 1/4-1/2 inch thick. Preheat oven to meduim-high (400° F., 200° C.).

5. Transfer the dough to a baking sheet and allow to rise for some 10 minutes.

6. With your fingertips, make indentations across the top of the bread, 1 1/4 inch apart. Sprinkle with olive oil (allow to run into indentations) and salt. Bake in preheated oven for 20-25 minutes, or until golden. Serve warm, fresh from the oven.

ONION AND ROSEMARY BREAD

focaccia con cipolle e rosemarino

INGREDIENTS:

Focaccia dough (page 40)
1/2 cup olive oil
1/2 tablespoon coarse (kosher) salt
1 large onion, thinly sliced
1 tablespoon rosemary leaves

1. Prepare the dough as in previous recipe (Focaccia bread). Roll out, place on the baking sheet, and press a grid of indentations. Preheat oven to a meduim-high temperature (400° F., 200° C.).

2. Heat olive oil in a frying pan, add onion and fry lightly, until transparent.

3. Spread fried onions and the oil over the dough, sprinkle with rosemary and salt and bake for 20-25 minutes. Serve warm.

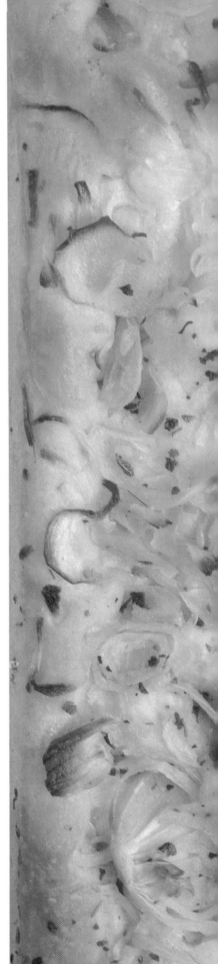

One of those simple sights, filling the house with delicious, mouthwatering smells

PIZZA DOUGH

INGREDIENTS:

2 cups plain flour
1/2 oz. fresh yeast
A little salt
2 tablespoons olive oil

1. Dissolve the yeast in 1/2 cup lukewarm water.

2. Place flour in a large bowl and make a well in the center. Pour the yeast mixture into the well, mix well and cover with a damp towel. Allow to rise at room temperature for about 30 minutes.

3. Add another 1/2 cup lukewarm water and the olive oil. Mix until the dough loses its stickiness. If the dough retains its stickiness, add a little flour.

4. Transfer the dough to a lightly floured working surface and knead thoroughly for about 5 minutes. Gather into a ball, cover with a damp towel, and allow to rise for about 30 minutes.

PIZZA MARGHERITA

INGREDIENTS:

Pizza dough (p. 42)
6 ripe tomatoes
2-3 tablespoons virgin olive oil
1 large mozzarella cheese, thinly sliced
8 anchovy fillets
12 black olives, pitted and halved
Salt and freshly ground black pepper
6 coarsely chopped basil leaves

1. Preheat oven to high (475° F., 230° C.). Roll the dough to a circle about 1/4 inch thick. Transfer to a baking sheet.

2. Dip the tomatoes in boiling water for a few seconds, peel, and chop coarsely.

3. Brush the dough with olive oil and cover with the chopped tomatoes.

4. Arrange cheese slices, anchovies, and olives evenly on top of the tomatoes. Season with salt and pepper, sprinkle with basil leaves and olive oil.

5. Bake in preheated oven for 20-30 minutes, until the dough is brown and crisp at the edges.

PEPPER PIZZA

peperoni pizza

INGREDIENTS:

Pizza dough (p. 42)
1 sweet red pepper
1 yellow pepper
4 tablespoons virgin olive oil
2 chopped garlic cloves
4 chopped anchovy fillets
1 large mozzarella cheese, coarsely crumbled or chopped
Salt and freshly ground black pepper
1 tablespoon chopped oregano leaves

1. Roll out dough to a circle about 1/4 inch thick and transfer to a baking sheet. Preheat oven to high (475° F., 230° C.).

2. Halve peppers, remove seeds and slice into 1/2 inch strips. Brush with olive oil.

3. Arrange the peppers atop the dough. Sprinkle with garlic, anchovies and the crumbled cheese. Season with salt and pepper. Sprinkle with olive oil and the oregano.

4. Bake in preheated oven for 20-30 minutes, or until dough is brown and crisp at the edge.

SAUSAGE PIZZA (1)

pizza salcicce

INGREDIENTS:

Pizza dough (p. 42)
1 lb. sharp Italian sausage
8-10 dried porcini mushrooms,
  soaked in warm water for at
  least 30 minutes
2 tablespoons chopped parsley
⅓ cup quality olive oil

1. Roll out dough to a circle about ¼ inch thick. Transfer to a baking sheet. Preheat oven to high (475° F., 230° C.).

2. Slice sausage diagonally into ¼ inch thick slices.

3. Take the mushrooms from the water and squeeze out excess moisture.

4. Arrange sausage slices atop the dough. Cover with mushrooms and parsely and sprinkle with olive oil.

5. Bake for 20-30 minutes, or until dough is brown and crisp around the edges.

MUSHROOM PIZZA

pizza funghi

INGREDIENTS:

Pizza dough (p. 42)
5 oz. fresh button mushrooms
8-10 dried porcini mushrooms,
  soaked for at least 30 minutes
  in warm water
Salt and freshly ground black
  pepper
10 coarsely chopped basil leaves
2 finely chopped garlic cloves
¼ cup quality olive oil
1 large ball mozzarella, grated or
  chopped

1. Roll the dough to a circle about ¼ inch thick and transfer to a baking sheet. Preheat oven to high (475° F., 230° C.).

2. Slice fresh mushrooms. Remove dried mushrooms from water, squeeze out excess moisture and chop coarsely.

3. Mix the mushrooms, basil, garlic, and olive oil. Season with salt and pepper to taste.

4. Spread mushroom mixture on dough and sprinkle with mozzarella.

5. Bake for 20-30 minutes, or until dough is brown and crisp around the edges.

SAUSAGE PIZZA (2)

INGREDIENTS:

Pizza dough (p. 42)
6 ripe tomatoes, peeled, seeded and coarsely chopped
1 lb. sharp Italian sausage, thinly sliced
1 tablespoon finely chopped basil leaves
Salt and freshly ground black pepper
3 tablespoons olive oil

1. Preheat oven to high (475° F., 230° C.).

2. Roll out dough to a circle about 1/4 inch thick. Transfer to a baking sheet.

3. Spread chopped tomatoes on dough, and arrange sliced sausage evenly on top. Sprinkle with basil. Season with salt and pepper to taste and olive oil.

4. Bake for 20-30 minutes, or until dough is brown and crisp around the edges.

SPINACH PIZZA

INGREDIENTS:

Pizza dough (p. 42)
1 lb. fresh spinach, cleaned
3 oz. fat goats or sheep cheese, crumbled
2 chopped garlic cloves
Salt and freshly ground black pepper
A pinch of ground nutmeg
2-3 tablespoons quality olive oil

1. Preheat oven to high (475° F., 230° C.).

2. Roll out dough to a circle about 1/2 inch thick. Transfer to a baking sheet.

3. Cook the spinach in boiling salted water. Remove from saucepan, drain, and rinse under running water. Squeeze well to remove as much moisture as possible and chop coarsely.

4. Put spinach in a bowl, add crumbled cheese, garlic, and nutmeg. Season with salt and pepper, and mix.

5. Spread spinach mixture on dough and sprinkle with olive oil.

6. Bake for 20-30 minutes, or until dough is brown and crisp around the edges.

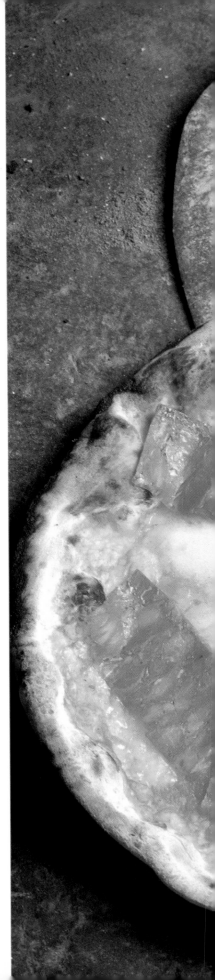

OLIVE AND SPINACH TART

INGREDIENTS:

DOUGH:

2 cups plain white flour
A pinch of salt
½ cup quality olive oil
1 egg

FILLING:

1 lb. spinach, rinsed thoroughly
¼ cup olive oil
1 finely chopped onion
1 chopped garlic clove
1 egg
3 tablespoons cream
Salt and freshly ground black
  pepper
2 sprigs fresh thyme, or
  1 tablespoon dried thyme
5 oz. pitted black olives, halved

1. To make dough: Put flour, salt, oil and egg in a food-processor fitted with the plastic blade and work until uniform. Gather into a ball, wrap in plastic and chill for about 1 hour. (Add cold water if dough seems too dry).

2. Preheat oven to medium (350° F., 180° C.). To make the filling, cook spinach in boiling salt water for about 3 minutes. Drain, rinse under running water and squeeze well to remove as much moisture as possible. Chop coarsely.

3. Heat the olive oil in a frying pan and sauté onion and garlic until the onion is transparent.

4. In a separate bowl, mix the spinach, egg and cream with the onion and garlic and season with salt and pepper. If using dried thyme, add it as well.

5. Roll the dough to a ½ inch thick circle. Press the dough into a tart pan, cut off excess dough around the edges, and prick surface with a fork.

6. Pour the spinach filling over the dough and spread evenly.

7. Arrange the olive halves on top of the filling, and if using fresh thyme sprigs, use to garnish.

8. Bake for about 45 minutes, until set.

EGGPLANT AND MOZZARELLA TART

torta di melanzane e mozzarella

INGREDIENTS:

DOUGH:

2 cups plain flour
A pinch of salt
½ cup quality olive oil
1 egg

FILLING:

2 eggplants
¾ cup quality olive oil
6 ripe tomatoes, peeled and
  coarsely chopped
2 chopped garlic cloves
1 large mozzarella, ball thinly sliced
1 handful of finely chopped fresh
  basil
2 handfuls finely chopped parsley

*Salt and freshly ground black
pepper*

1. To make dough, put flour, salt,
oil and egg in a food-processor
fitted with the plastic blade and
work until blended. If too dry add a
little cold water. Gather into a ball,
wrap in plastic and chill for about 1
hour.

2. Slice eggplants into ¼ inch
slices, sprinkle with salt, and set
aside for half an hour. Wipe dry.

3. Preheat oven to medium
(350° F., 180° C.). To make filling,
heat olive oil in a frying pan and fry
the salted and dried eggplants until
lightly golden.

4. Roll out dough to a ½ inch thick
circle. Press the dough into a tart
pan, cut off excess dough around
edges, and prick surface with a
fork.

5. Spread a third of the chopped
tomatoes on dough, cover with half
the eggplant slices and some garlic,
then half the mozzarella. Sprinkle
with a little olive oil, basil, parsley,
salt and pepper. Arrange a second
layer of eggplant slices and cover
with remaining tomatoes.

6. Bake for about 40 minutes.

SWISS CHARD TART

torta di bietole

INGREDIENTS:

DOUGH:

2 cups plain flour
A pinch of salt
½ cup quality olive oil
1 egg

FILLING:

¼ cup quality olive oil
1 onion, finely chopped
2 chopped garlic cloves
3 oz. button mushrooms, rinsed
 and sliced
1 lb. swiss chard leaves, rinsed
 thoroughly and coarsely chopped
2 tablespoons chopped marjoram
Salt and freshly ground black
 pepper
½ lb. ricotta cheese
2 eggs

1. To make dough, put flour, salt,
oil, and egg in a food-processor
fitted with the plastic blade, and
work until blended. If too dry, add a
little cold water. Gather into a ball,
wrap in plastic and chill for about 1
hour. Preheat oven to medium
(350° F., 180° C.).

2. For the filling, heat the oil in a
large frying pan and sauté the
chopped onion and garlic until the
onion becomes transparent.

3. Add the sliced mushrooms and
fry for about 1 minute. Add
chopped swiss chard leaves,
marjoram, salt and pepper to taste,
stir well, remove from fire, and
transfer to a bowl.

4. Add ricotta and eggs to the
swiss chard mixture and mix well.

5. Roll the dough to a ½ inch thick
circle. Press the dough into a tart
pan, cut off excess dough around
the edges and prick surface with a
fork. Pour filling into case.

6. Bake for about 45 minutes.
Serve hot.

Spinach may be substituted for
Swiss chard.

49

"**A** true cuisine can be measured by its soups," according to Fabio Pizzi. Fabio is the owner of a marvelous Florentine restaurant called "Cibreo". Plump and cheerful, with roguish eyes and a luxurious mustache, he strolls among his patrons in a pink striped shirt covered with a white apron. He chatters ceaselessly, laughs uproariously, and scowls at his waiters while firing rapid instructions at them.

"The French," says Fabio, "have the best restaurants. But we have the finest cuisine. Look at their soups, then look at ours..." he adds knowingly. One may argue the validity of Fabio's theory, but the yellow pepper soup we ate at his restaurant was simply superb. Creamy, rich, pale yellow and delicious.

Like many Italians, Fabio takes his soup seriously. Not a haphazard combination of aged vegetables, thrown into water and boiled within an inch of their lives. Italian soup making usually starts with sofrito – gentle frying of aromatic vegetables. Chopped carrot, onion, celery, and garlic fried in olive oil. A serious cook would then add clear stock, a less serious cook would add water, but noone would add powdered soup.

The vegetables added at the next stage are never overcooked. They retain their flavour, texture and color. The right amount of herbs and spices would then contribute the "sting", and noodles are added to some of the soups to give them "body". A little good olive oil is nearly always added at the last moment, to carry the soup to the heights so eloquently praised by Fabio.

Some of the soups are thick: those made of dried pulses, beans, chickpeas and pearl barley. These are country soups, eaten with country bread and olive oil. Then there are the more refined vegetable soups of the minestrone family. They are tasty, colorful, and pleasing to the eye. And there are the creamy soups, worked to a smooth puree, and enriched with butter or milk.

Each soup has its own unique trait, each vegetable its characteristic flavor, each region its local ingredients. The soups of Puglia region, in the south, are based on the sea-rich, delicious fish soups – made of a variety of fish and shellfish. Some are made with tomatoes, but all of them contain garlic, olive oil and herbs. Such a soup can be a full meal in itself. In the northern regions you will find the clear soups, based on veal or chicken stock, or a combination of both.

BARLEY SOUP

INGREDIENTS:

10 oz. beans, (preferably dried
 Borlotto beans)
½ cup olive oil
1 large onion, finely chopped
1 diced carrot
2 thinly sliced celery stalks
2-4 chopped garlic cloves
1 stick cinnamon
5 fresh sage leaves
4 tomatoes, peeled and chopped
4 cups stock or water
10 oz. barley, well rinsed
Salt and freshly ground black
 pepper

1. Soak beans overnight in plenty of water.

2. Cook the beans in 5 cups of water over a low flame for about 1½ hours, or until very tender.

3. Heat olive oil in a saucepan, add onion, carrot and celery and sauté over a low heat for about 10 minutes. Add garlic, cinnamon, sage and tomatoes and fry a further 5 minutes. Remove from heat and remove cinnamon stick.

4. Place beans in a food-processor fitted with the steel blade, add the sautéd vegetables and work to a smooth puree. Return to the large pot and add stock or water.

5. Add pearl barley, season with salt and pepper to taste, and bring to a boil. Reduce flame to minimum and cook for about an hour. If the soup thickens too much, dilute it with a little water.

This should be a very thick soup, served hot but not boiling, with plenty of quality olive oil dripped on top and accompanied by farm bread.

A soup to be eaten, not drunk, accompanied by thick slices of Italian bread and a heavy red wine.

FENNEL SOUP

zuppa di finoccio

INGREDIENTS:

4 fennel bulbs
1/3 cup virgin olive oil
6 cups clear stock
Salt and freshly ground black
    pepper
3 large tablespoons finely chopped
    parsley

1. Clean fennel, remove and discard core.

2. Dice fennel.

3. Heat the oil in a large pot, add diced fennel and sauté, over a low flame, for about 10 minutes. Stir occasionally.

4. Add stock and bring to a boil. Reduce heat and cook, uncovered, for about half an hour. Season with salt and pepper to taste.

5. Pour into individual serving bowls, sprinkle with chopped parsley and serve.

SPINACH SOUP

paparot

INGREDIENTS:

1 lb. spinach, thorougly cleaned
2 oz. butter
1 finely chopped onion
2 chopped garlic cloves
1 tablespoon flour
5 cups clear stock or water
Salt and freshly ground black
    pepper
Grated nutmeg
2 tablespoons cornmeal

1. Cook the spinach in boiling salted water for about 3 minutes. Drain, rinse under running water and squeeze well to remove as much moisture as possible. Chop in a food-processor fitted with a steel blade.

2. Melt butter in a large pot, add onion and garlic, and sauté until the onion becomes transparent.

3. Add flour, stir, and then add the spinach.

4. Add stock or water, season with salt, pepper and nutmeg, and bring to a boil. Add cornmeal and cook, uncovered, for about half an hour. Stir occasionally while cooking, adjust seasoning, and serve.

BREAD AND TOMATO SOUP

pappa al pomodoro

INGREDIENTS:

6 slices Italian-style bread
4 tablespoons quality olive oil
2 chopped garlic cloves
1 small hot chili pepper (optional)
2 lb. ripe tomatoes, peeled and
    chopped
10 finely chopped basil leaves
Salt and freshly ground black
    pepper
6 cups clear stock or water

1. Lightly toast bread.

2. Heat oil in a large suacepan, add garlic and chili pepper (if using) and fry gently, stirring constantly.

3. Add tomatoes, basil, salt and pepper. Cook for about 5 minutes, stirring occasionally.

4. Add stock or water and bring to a boil.

5. Add bread and cook over a low heat, stirring constantly, for about 15 minutes, or until bread crumbles in the soup.

6. Pour into individual serving bowls and sprinkle generously with olive oil.

The bread makes a very thick soup. For a thinner soup, use a little less bread.

ONION SOUP

zuppa di cipolle

INGREDIENTS:

$1/2$ cup quality olive oil
2 lb. onions, peeled and thinly
    sliced
2-3 thinly sliced garlic cloves
2 stalks celery, thinly sliced
2 large tablespoons basil leaves,
    finely chopped
4 ripe tomatoes, peeled and finely
    chopped
5 cups clear stock
Salt and freshly ground black
    pepper
1 lb. puff pastry (optional)

1. Put olive oil in a large pot. Add onion, garlic, celery and basil and sauté for 10-15 minutes, until onion is transparent. Stir occasionally, using a wooden spoon.

2. Add chopped tomatoes, stir and cook another 2 minutes.

3. Add stock, season with salt and pepper to taste and bring to a boil. Cover, reduce heat to minimum, and cook for about 45 minutes.

The soup may be served at this stage.

VARIATION: Prepare 6 deep, ovenproof individual soup bowls. Preheat oven to high.

Roll out puff pastry thinly and cut out 6 circles, 1 inch larger than the diameter of a soup bowl.

Brush the outer sides of soup bowls with beaten egg, about 1 inch from the rim.

Fill each bowl with hot soup, cover with a pastry circle, and press onto the rim. Brush pastry with beaten egg, and bake for 10-15 minutes, until pastry is evenly browned. To eat, break pastry cover into the soup.

CREAMED VEGETABLE SOUP WITH PESTO

minestrone genovese al pesto

INGREDIENTS:

½ cup dried white beans
⅓ cup virgin olive oil
1 large onion, finely chopped
2 diced carrots
2 stalks celery, thinly sliced
5 cups water
½ lb. spinach leaves, thoroughly cleaned
2 potatoes, peeled and diced
1 sliced leek
A bunch of parsley
1 bay leaf
Salt and freshly ground black pepper
6 tablespoons pesto sauce (p. 82)
6 tablespoons virgin olive oil
2 oz. pine nuts

1. Soak beans overnight in plenty of water.

2. Heat the olive oil in a large pot, add onion, carrot and celery and sauté over a low heat for about 10 minutes.

3. Add water, spinach, potatoes, leek, parsley, bay leaf and the soaked beans. Season with salt and pepper to taste, bring to a boil, reduce heat to minimum and cook for about an hour, or until the beans are very tender.

4. Strain soup. Reserve liquids, and transfer the vegetables to a food-processor fitted with a steel blade. Work to a smooth puree.

5. Return pureed vegetables to the pan, add reserved cooking liquids and stir well.

6. Add pesto and stir.

7. Pour into individual serving bowls, garnish each bowl with a tablespoon of oil and some pine nuts and serve at once.

This soup is eaten warm rather than steaming hot.

See what a little olive oil can do... a few drops of olive oil, and the soup soars to heavenly heights.

BEAN SOUP

zuppa di fagioli

INGREDIENTS:

2 cups dried white beans
2 carrots, peeled and halved
1 large onion, quartered
2 celery stalks, cut into strips
1 bunch parsley
1 small sprig rosemary
Salt and freshly ground black
*   pepper*
4 chopped garlic cloves
1/3 cup olive oil
2 tablespoons finely chopped
*   parsley*

1. Soak beans overnight in plenty of water.

2. Place beans, carrots, onion, celery, parsley, and rosemary in a large pan. Add 6 cups of water and bring to a boil. Reduce heat to minimum, cover, and cook for about 2 hours, or until the beans are tender.

3. Remove and discard parsley and rosemary. Strain and reserve liquids. Transfer half of the cooked vegetables to a food-processor fitted with a steel blade and work to a smooth puree. Return puree, whole vegetables and liquids to pan and stir. Add a little water if needed. Season with salt and pepper.

4. Heat the olive oil in a frying pan. Add the garlic and fry until golden. Add the parsley and stir. Add hot garlic oil to soup, stir and serve hot.

"WOODCUTTERS" CHICKPEA SOUP

zuppa di leci

We ate this soup in Montalcino. It was prepared the previous day to feed 50 workers who came to build wood cabins in the vicinity.

INGREDIENTS:

8 oz. dried chickpeas (garbanzo
*   beans)*
1/4 cup olive oil
1 large Spanish onion, finely
*   chopped*
4 garlic cloves, chopped
2 tomatoes, peeled and finely
*   chopped*
1 tablespoon chopped rosemary
Salt and freshly ground black
*   pepper*
6 cups clear stock or water
3 oz. penne, or other short pasta,
*   cooked and drained*

1. Soak chickpeas overnight in plenty of water.

2. Heat the olive oil in a large pan. Add the onion and garlic and fry until the onion becomes transparent. Add tomatoes and sauté for another 2 minutes.

3. Add chickpeas, rosemary and stock or water. Season with salt and pepper to taste.

4. Bring to a boil, cover, reduce heat to minimum and cook for 1 1/2 hours, or until the chickpeas are soft.

5. Add the pasta and serve immediately.

PEA SOUP

zuppa crema di piselli

INGREDIENTS:

1/4 cup olive oil
1 finely chopped onion
2 oz. smoked beef, thinly sliced
    and cut into strips
1 celery stalk, thinly sliced
1 lb. fresh or frozen peas
4 cups clear stock or water
1/4 cup chopped parsley
Salt and freshly ground black
    pepper to taste
1/2 cup (non-dairy) cream

1. Put the olive oil in a large pot,
add onion and sauté until
transparent.

2. Add smoked meat and celery
and sauté for another 5 minutes.

3. Add peas and stir for about a
minute.

4. Add stock or water and parsley,
bring to a boil, reduce heat to
minimum and cook for about
20 minutes, or until peas are
tender.

5. Strain soup and reserve 1 cup of
the cooking liquid. Transfer
vegetables and reserved liquids to
a food-processor fitted with a steel
blade and work to a smooth puree.
Return to the pan. Bring to a boil
and season with salt and pepper.

6. Add non-dairy cream, stir, heat
and serve.

YELLOW PEPPER SOUP

zuppa di peperone giallo

INGREDIENTS:

1/3 cup olive oil
1 large onion, chopped
5 cups stock or water
4 large, firm yellow peppers,
    seeded and diced
2 potatoes, peeled and diced
Salt and freshly ground black
    pepper
3 oz. softened butter
6 tablespoons olive oil

1. Heat olive oil in a large pan, add
onion and sauté for about 10
minutes.

2. Add stock or water, peppers and
potatoes and bring to a boil.
Reduce heat to a minimum and
cook for about 30 minutes.

3. Strain soup and reserve liquids.
Transfer vegetables to a food-
processor fitted with a steel blade
and work to a smooth puree. Press
through a sieve into the pan (the
peels will remain in the sieve) and
add reserved liquids. Season with
salt and pepper to taste and bring
to a boil. Remove from heat.

4. Gradually stir in the butter, a
tablespoon at a time.

5. Pour into individual soup bowls,
add a tablespoon of olive oil to
each bowl, and serve.

MINESTRONE

INGREDIENTS:

1/2 cup dried white beans
1/3 cup quality olive oil
1 chopped onion
2 thinly sliced garlic cloves
2 oz. smoked beef, cut into strips
4 tablespoons mixed herbs (basil,
    sage, marjoram, parsley, thyme)
4 tomatoes, peeled and chopped
1/2 cup dry red wine
6 cups stock or water
2 carrots, peeled and diced
2 sliced celery stalks
1 sliced leek
Salt and freshly ground black
    pepper
1 cup short, broad pasta, cooked

1. Soak beans overnight in plenty
of water. Drain.

2. Heat oil in a large pan, add
onion and garlic and sauté for a
few minutes. Add smoked beef and
herbs and sauté for another
3 minutes.

3. Add tomatoes and stir for a few
minutes. Add wine, bring to a boil
and allow to boil for 2-3 minutes.

4. Add beans and stock or water,
bring to a boil and cook, covered,
for 1 hour, or until beans are
tender.

5. Add remaining vegetables and
cook a further 20 minutes. Season
with salt and pepper, add cooked
pasta, stir, and serve hot, with
bread. The soup may be garnished
with a tablespoon of pesto (see
page 82).

Down every street, up every alley, you will find the Italians sitting in large groups and making that turning motion with their fork, wrapping the noodles around it, making the sucking sounds, and the noodles are slurped in as elegantly as possible under the circumstances.

One may forget the antipasti, one may omit the main course of meat or fish, but there is hardly an Italian meal which does not include pasta. The pasta may be the highlight of a large family dinner, and arrive at the table in an enormous bowl, redolent of garlic, from which the noodles are ladled on to the plates, soaking in heavy sauce. Happiest is he who is fortunate enough to be the last – he can eat straight from the bowl, sprinkle the grated Parmesan on the noodles and the sauce at the bottom of the bowl, and wash it all down with a large glass of red wine.

In a fancy restaurant, pasta may be served as a light and refined first course – such as half a dozen delicate ravioli, stuffed with a light filling and covered with transparent sauce.

Pasta may also constitute a light, informal lunch, accompanied by a glass of light white wine, and served smothered in shellfish, or topped with a green basil sauce. The pasta itself can be delicate, rolled out thinly and cooked for only a few minutes, or thick and heavy. It can be made by a housewife, rolled with a wooden rolling pin, cut with a kitchen knife, and shaped with her fingertips; or it can come, elegantly packaged, from a factory.

The controversy surrounding the origins of pasta is old, and will probably go on forever. Was it Marco Polo who brought noodles from China, or does the barely legible inscription in the ancient writings suggest that pasta has existed in Italy since the dawn of history? Actually, who cares? as long as there is pasta!

Spaghetti – round-sectioned, thin, long noodles.
Macaroni – round-sectioned hollow noodles, may be thick and short or thinner and longer.
Penne – literally, "feathers". Short, thick, hollow noodles, cut diagonally.
Fettuccine – (or tagliatelle) long, broad and totally flat noodles.
Gnocchi – soft, spongy, potato-based dumplings.
Ravioli – circles, triangles or squares, stuffed with cheese or other fillings.
Tortellini – stuffed dough, generally filled with meat.
Lasagne – layers of pasta sheets and fillings, baked together.

There are two kinds of pasta: fresh, a freshly made dough rolled out and cut into various shapes, and cooked in boiling water shortly after preparation; and dried pasta, which is dried out in special ovens and therefore keeps longer. Pasta quality is determined by the type and quality of the flour (dried pasta should always be made from durum wheat). Only fresh pasta uses eggs.

In addition to noodles, there are also stuffed fresh pastas, which include ravioli, tortellini and cannelloni. Strips of thin dough, in various shapes, filled with different fillings. Depending on their size and thickness, they are boiled for a specific length of time, then topped with sauce. Lasagne is the same thin strips layered with sauce.
Cooking is critical. Pasta should be dropped into well salted boiling water. The water must be plentiful (about 2½ quarts for each pound of pasta). Pasta should not be overcooked. The Italians define properly cooked pasta "al dente" – soft enough to eat, but hard enough to chew on.

It is difficult to determine exactly how long pasta should be cooked. It depends on the type, thickness, and heat. Fresh pasta requires much shorter cooking than dried; thick pasta calls for longer cooking than this; The cooking time of stuffed pasta varies according to the type of filling and its quantity. To determine whether pasta is cooked, simply take out a noodle or two and bite it. When ready, pour immediately into a large sieve placed over the sink, and drain. There is no need to rinse it.

It is usually preferable to have the sauce ready when the pasta is cooked. Mix and eat.

The recipes in this chapter are simple suggestions. Recipes can be crossed; a pasta from one recipe can certainly be combined with a sauce from another. The possibilities are endless, and the pleasure is all yours.

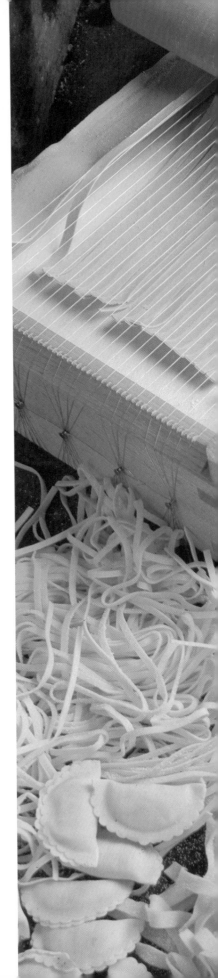

Dried pasta (above), in an
old-fashioned factory; fresh
pasta (left). The spinach colors
the pasta green. The stringed,
wooden frame, called a
"guitar", determines the size
and width of the pasta.

PASTA DOUGH

About 1½ lb., 6 servings

INGREDIENTS:

1 lb. flour
5-6 eggs
1 level teaspoon salt
1 tablespoon olive oil

1. Pile the flour into a rather low mound on a wide working surface, and in the center make a well large enough to contain all the eggs comfortably.

2. Lightly beat eggs in a bowl.

3. Carefully pour eggs, salt, and oil into the well.

4. Using the fingers of one hand, gather flour from the edges of the well and slowly add to the eggs. Use the other hand to support the rims of the well and prevent eggs from "leaking". Continue until eggs and flour are well mixed.

5. Knead the pasta, folding it on itself and pressing with base of palms, for 5-7 minutes, to make a smooth, elastic and shiny dough.

6. Gather into a ball, cover with a damp cloth and allow to rest for an hour.

* Colourful, flavored pasta can be made with the following additions:

HERB PASTA: Finely chop 1 tablespoon fresh basil, 1 tablespoon fresh parsley, 1 tablespoon sage. Add to dough ingredients and knead. The resulting pasta is greenish, aromatic and especially tasty.

GREEN PASTA: Cook 5 oz. spinach in boiling water for 5 minutes, drain and squeeze to remove as much moisture as possible. Work to a smooth puree, using a food-processor, add to dough ingredients and knead together. The resulting pasta is green and has a delicate spinach flavour.

RED PASTA: Wash a medium beetroot and cook in salted water for 45 minutes. Rinse and peel. Work to a smooth puree, using a food-processor. Add to dough ingredients and knead together. The resulting pasta is red, and has a delicate beetroot flavour.

ORANGE SAFFRON PASTA: Place ½ a teaspoon saffron strands in a small bowl, and add about ¼ cup hot water. Allow to stand for 10 minutes, add strands and liquids to dough ingredients and knead. The resulting pasta is red, and has a delicate saffron fragrance.

1 *Add flour to the center of the well with one hand, while supporting the rim with the other hand.*

2 *Continue until flour and eggs are well mixed.*

3 *Knead dough with base of palms.*

4 *After 5-7 minutes the dough is smooth and elastic.*

CUTTING FRESH DOUGH INTO NOODLES

1. Divide the dough into two balls.

2. Place 1 ball on a floured board and roll out as thinly as possible. During rolling, sprinkle a little flour on dough and rolling pin to prevent sticking.

3. When dough is suitably thin, sprinkle a little flour on top. Lift dough on one side and fold 1-1½ inches towards the center. Continue to roll towards the center, until half the dough is folded. Repeat from the other side.

4. Using a large, sharp knife, cut folded dough into strips about ¼ inch wide.

5. Insert a long knife under the folded strips and lift up so that the noodles unfold.

1 *Roll out dough on a floured board.*

4 *Continue folding from the edge to the center, then repeat on the other side.*

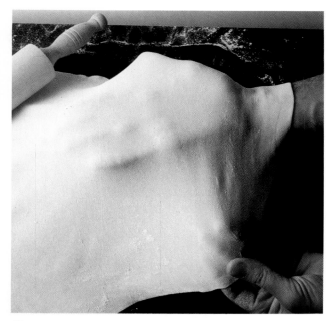

2 *Roll out as thinly as possible.*

3 *Sprinkle rolled dough with flour, and fold 1-1¼ inches inwards.*

5 *Using a sharp knife, cut folded dough into strips.*

6 *Insert a sharp knife underneath the center of the folded dough, lift up and unfold the noodles.*

CUTTING PASTA ON A PASTA MACHINE

There are several simple devices designed to cut and shape pasta:
A grooved rolling pin. When rolled over the pasta dough in a steady, continuous movement, the dough is cut into thin, uniform strips.
A wooden frame strung with variously spaced wires. The dough, rolled out thinly, is placed over the wires. It is then rolled again with a rolling pin, which cuts it into strips.

The most efficient device is a simple, manual pasta cutter, that rolls out the dough to the desired thickness and cuts it to the desired width:

1. Press pasta dough with the palm of your hand, to flatten it a little.

2. Position the two drums of the pasta cutter as wide apart as possible and insert dough. Roll out. Repeat several times, to knead the dough.

3. Adjust the drums to reduce the space between them, insert dough and roll out.

4. Repeat inserting and flattening dough until it forms an elongated, thin strip.

5. Adjust the cutting wires to desired width, insert dough between cutting drums, roll out and the pasta is ready.

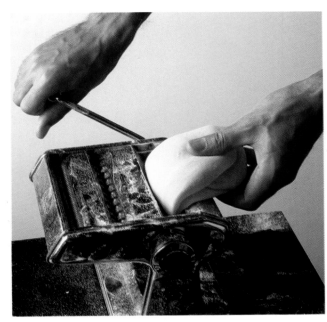

1 *Roll dough between drums spaced as widely as possible.*

4 *Insert the strip between the cutting drums, adjusted to the desired width, and start rolling.*

2 Bring drums closer and roll dough again.

3 Continue adjusting the drums closer and closer, and rolling out the dough to a thin, elongated strip.

5 Roll until the cut pasta slips out of the cutter.

COOKING PASTA

Cooking pasta, both homemade and store-bought, is as important as making it.

Follow a few basic rules, and your pasta will be cooked to the right texture.

QUANTITY OF WATER: Pasta should be cooked in plenty of boiling, salted water, in a large pan. The quantity of dough in the recipe above (about 1½ lb, 6 servings) requires about 5 quarts of water. If cooked in less, the pasta might be sticky. Add a level tablespoon of salt and a tablespoon of olive oil to the water. The water must boil before the pasta is added. While cooking, the water should continue to boil gently. Stir pasta occasionally to prevent its sticking. Place the pasta in the water when it is thoroughly boiling, and after it is inside, make sure it continues to simmer, not boiling wildly, but definitely boiling!

COOKING TIME is most important. Unfortunately, although pasta does require a precise cooking time, it cannot be rigidly stated. The length of cooking depends on the pasta, its thickness and its size. Thick pasta needs to be cooked longer than thin pasta. The basic rule is never to undercook it, and even more important, never to overcook it – the Italian term is "al dente" ("to the tooth", firm enough to be slightly resistant to the bite, yet soft enough to eat). It should be soft, yet firm enough to the touch. This is a skill acquired through time and experience. When the pasta is cooked, it is transferred immediately to a large, wide colander.

THE SAUCE should be prepared in advance, so that the cooked pasta can be topped with it, and served at once.

1 Fill a large pot with water, add oil and salt and bring to the boil. Add pasta and stir.

2 Using a wooden spoon, transfer cooked pasta to drain in a colander.

STUFFED PASTAS

Ravioli, tortellini, cannelloni, lasagne – these are names for different shapes of pasta, stuffed with varied fillings. Most are cooked like ordinary pastas and served with a sauce, some are baked.
Naturally, it is the filling that gives them their singularity, therefore it must be tasty and made from the finest ingredients.

TORTELLINI

1. On a floured board, roll out the dough as thinly as possible.

2. Cut into 2½×2½ inch squares.

3. Place a square with one of the corners facing you. Place a little of the filling o the half nearer you, fold the nearest corner to cover the filling, then fold again so that only the farthest corner remains flat.
4. Hold both side corners and bend backwards (away from the unfolded corner). Press both together.

* Ravioli and tortellini require longer cooking than unfilled pastas, because of the filling – 10-12 minutes, depending on thickness, size, and the type of filling used.

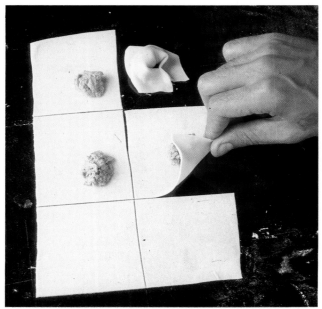

1 Place a teaspoon of filling in one corner of the square, Fold dough over to cover filling , then fold again in the same direction.

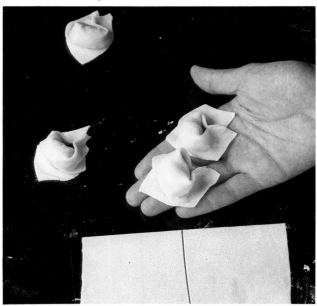

2 Leave opposite corner unfolded, to form a triangle. Pull the two points at the base backwards, and press to seal.

RAVIOLI

1. Divide dough into two balls and roll out two equal strips, as thin as possible.

2. On one strip, place single teaspoons of the filling, evenly spaced.

3. Moisten the dough between the mounds of filling with a little water. Cover with second strip of dough.

4. Using your fingertips, press strips together around filling to seal it in.

5. Using a sharp knife or a pastry cutter, cut into equal-sized squares.

The dough may also be cut into circles, with a sharp cookie cutter, or a glass. Each circle is then filled, folded in half and sealed.

1 *Place teaspoonfuls of the filling on the dough, evenly spaced.*

4 *Press both strips together in the spaces between the mounds of filling.*

2 *Moisten the spaces between the mounds of filling with a little water.*

3 *Cover the filling with the remaining strip.*

5 *Cut into equal-sized squares in the spaces between mounds of filling.*

6 *The dough can also be cut into circles, which are then filled and folded in half.*

POTATO GNOCCHI

gnocchi di patate

INGREDIENTS:

2 lb. potatoes
2½ cups plain white flour
2 eggs
1 oz. softened butter
Salt and freshly ground black
 pepper

1. Peel potatoes and cook in salted water until tender. Drain well, return to pot, and shake pot over flame to dry all traces of moisture.

2. Put potatoes through a ricer and mash to a smooth puree. Transfer to a bowl.

3. Add flour, eggs, and butter, season with salt and pepper, and knead to a soft, uniform dough. If dough is too soft, add a little more flour. Chill for several hours.

4. On a floured board, roll dough to a sausage-shape about the size of a finger, and cut into 1 inch pieces.

5. Cook for about 3 minutes in plenty of salted boiling water, until the gnocchi float to the surface. Remove from saucepan and drain.

Arrange cooked gnocchi in an oven-proof dish, top with grated Parmesan and a little butter, and broil for 2-3 minutes, until cheese melts.

FILLINGS FOR RAVIOLI AND TORTELLINI

A. CHEESE AND SPINACH FILLING

INGREDIENTS:

10 oz. fresh spinach, rinsed and
 cleaned
10 oz. ricotta cheese
3 oz. grated Parmesan
2 eggs
Salt and freshly ground black
 pepper

1. Cook spinach in boiling salted water for about 3 minutes. Remove from water, drain, rinse, and squeeze out as much moisture as possible. Chop coarsely.

2. In a bowl, mix ricotta, Parmesan, spinach, and eggs. Season with salt and pepper. Allow to cool before using.
The spinach may be omitted, in which case use only one egg.

B. MEAT FILLING

INGREDIENTS:

¼ cup olive oil
1 finely chopped onion
1 chopped garlic clove
8 oz. veal, cubed
3 oz. smoked beef, cubed
Salt and freshly ground black
 pepper
1 bay leaf
1 teaspoon dried rosemary or
 thyme, or a combination of both
½ cup dry white wine
8 oz. fresh spinach, cooked and
 coarsely chopped

1. Heat oil in a frying pan, add onion and garlic, and sauté until onion becomes transparent.

2. Add veal and beef, and fry for about 5 minutes.

3. Season with salt and pepper, add herbs and wine. Reduce heat to minimum, and cook, covered, for about 45 minutes.

4. Chop finely, add spinach and mix well.

Miranda is a plump, smiling Tuscan woman. The ravioli served in her restaurant may not be uniformly sized, but they are simply delicious. She also owns a small delicatesen, and a nice little hotel above the restaurant.

TORTELLINI WITH EGGS AND CREAM

INGREDIENTS:

1¹/₂ lb. tortellini (p. 75)
1 cup cream
2 egg yolks
Salt and freshly ground black
*   pepper*

1. Cook tortellini in a large saucepan, in plenty of water, with 1 teaspoon salt, for about 10 minutes (depending on size). Place in a large colander to drain, and transfer to a large bowl.

2. Place cream and yolks in a small bowl, beat lightly, and season with salt and pepper to taste.

3. Pour cream sauce on the hot tortellini and mix. Serve immediately.

TORTELLINI IN PINK SAUCE

tortellini rosa

INGREDIENTS:

1¹/₂ lb. tortellini (p. 75)

SAUCE:

6 large, ripe tomatoes
1 cup cream
Salt and freshly ground black
*   pepper*
2 tablespoons finely chopped
*   parsley*

1. To make the sauce: Scald tomatoes in boiling water, then peel. Cut in half and squeeze to remove seeds. Place in a food-processor fitted with a steel blade and work until smooth. Sieve. In a medium saucepan, heat cream to just below boiling point. Cook without boiling for 3 or 4 minutes, until slightly thickened.
Add tomato puree, season with salt and pepper, stir, and cook for about 3 minutes.

2. Cook tortellini in a large pan, with plenty of water and 1 teaspoon salt, for 8-10 minutes (depending on size). Drain in a large colander.

3. Transfer tortellini to a large bowl, carefully pour sauce on top, garnish with chopped parsley and serve.

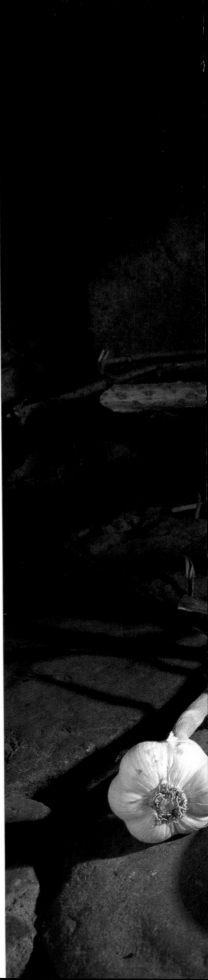

SPINACH GNOCCHI

gnocchi verdi

INGREDIENTS:

1¼ lb. fresh spinach, or 1 lb.
    frozen spinach
3 oz. butter
1 small onion
7 oz. fresh ricotta
Grated nutmeg
3 oz. grated Parmesan
2 eggs
1 egg yolk
1¼ cups plain white flour
Salt and freshly ground black
    pepper

1. Cook fresh spinach in boiling
salted water for about 3 minutes,
drain and rinse. Squeeze well and
chop; if using frozen spinach, thaw,
squeeze and chop.

2. Make a cross-shaped incision in
onion. Melt an ounce of the butter
in a frying pan, add onion and
spinach, and sauté over low heat
for about 6 minutes. Allow to cool
slightly.

3. Transfer spinach mixture to a
bowl, add the ricotta, nutmeg, half
of the Parmesan, the eggs, the yolk
and 1 cup of flour. Knead well and
season with salt and pepper to
taste. Cover and chill for several
hours, or even overnight.

4. Shape dough into small balls and
roll in flour.

5. Fill a large saucepan with water,
add 1 teaspoon salt, and bring to a
boil. Slide gnocchi into boiling water
and cook until they float to the
surface (about 5 minutes). Transfer
to a colander, drain, and arrange in
an oven-proof dish.

6. Before serving, preheat oven to
medium-high (400° F., 200° C.). Dot
gnocchi with remaining butter, top
with Parmesan, and bake until
cheese and butter melt.

GNOCCHI WITH PESTO

gnocchi al pesto

INGREDIENTS:

1½ lb. potato gnocchi (p. 78)

SAUCE:

1 cup fresh basil leaves
4-8 peeled garlic cloves
3 oz. pine nuts
2 oz. finely grated Parmesan
¾ cup good virgin olive oil
Salt and freshly ground black
    pepper

1. Make the sauce: Place basil,
garlic, pine nuts, and cheese in a
food processor fitted with a steel
blade, and work to a smooth
puree. Slowly add oil and work unt
evenly blended. Transfer to a bowl,
using a spatula, and season with
salt and pepper.

2. Fill a large pan with water, add
1 teaspoon salt and bring to a boil
Slide gnocchi into boiling water and
cook until they float to the surface
(3-4 minutes). Transfer to a
colander and drain.

3. Serve gnocchi onto individual
serving dishes, place 2
tablespoonfuls of the pesto sauce
over each dish and serve.

* The gnocchi may be garnished
with a few pine nuts and basil
leaves.

*Soft, fluffy and rounded
Gnocchi are the only
potato-based pasta. The Pesto
sauce originated in Genoa, a
city of sailors. Once home,
after the long voyage and the
preserved foods, the sailors
relished the fresh herbs.*

A time honored tradition – the elders of the village gather every day in the local cafe.

SPAGHETTI IN OLIVE SAUCE

spaghetti alla olive

INGREDIENTS:

1½ lb. spaghetti

SAUCE:

5 oz. pitted black olives
4 anchovy fillets
½ cup quality olive oil
3 garlic cloves, chopped
4 tablespoons finely chopped dill (optional)
A pinch of freshly ground black pepper
A few sliced mushrooms (optional)

1. Make the sauce: Place olives and anchovies in a food-processor fitted with a steel blade and work to a smooth puree. Heat half the oil in a frying pan, add garlic, and fry lightly. Transfer all sauce ingredients to a bowl and mix well.

2. Bring a large pan of water with 1 teaspoon salt to a boil. Cook spaghetti (5-6 minutes if fresh, 10-12 minutes if dried). Transfer to a wide colander.

3. Transfer to a heated serving dish, add sauce, mix well and serve.

SPAGHETTI IN WALNUT SAUCE

spaghetti alla salsa di noci

INGREDIENTS:

1½ lb. spaghetti

SAUCE:

3 oz. shelled walnuts
1 oz. pine nuts
2 garlic cloves
3 tablespoons cream
¾ cup good olive oil
2 tablespoons grated Parmesan
Salt and freshly ground black
    pepper

1. Make the sauce: Place nuts, pine nuts, garlic and cream in a food-processor and work to a smooth puree. Gradually add olive oil into food-processor while still working. Add Parmesan, season with salt and pepper to taste and mix well. Transfer to a bowl.

2. Fill a large saucepan with water, add 1 teaspoon salt and bring to a boil. Cook spaghetti (5-6 minutes if fresh, 10-12 minutes if dried). Transfer to a wide colander.

3. Transfer to a heated serving dish, add sauce, mix well and serve.

Tortellini, Ravioli, Gnocchi – trays of freshly made pasta (left) and dried pasta of all shapes and colors.

SPAGHETTI WITH HERBS

spaghetti aromatici

INGREDIENTS:

1½ lb. spaghetti
½ cup olive oil
2 chopped garlic cloves
1 diced onion
3 tablespoons chopped parsley
1 tablespoon chopped basil
1 tablespoon thyme
1 tablespoon chopped sage
Salt and freshly ground black
    pepper

1. Fill a large saucepan with water, add 1 teaspoon salt and bring to a boil. Cook spaghetti (5-6 minutes if fresh, 10-12 minutes if dried). Drain in a wide colander and transfer to a bowl.

2. While spaghetti is cooking, heat olive oil in a frying pan, add garlic and onion, and sauté until onion is transparent.

3. Add all herbs and season with salt and pepper. Stir and remove from heat.

4. Pour contents of frying pan over spaghetti, mix and serve at once, accompanied by finely grated Parmesan cheese.

SPAGHETTI IN OLIVE OIL AND GARLIC SAUCE

spaghetti aglio e olio

INGREDIENTS:

1½ lb. spaghetti
½ cup olive oil
3-4 diced garlic cloves
Salt and freshly ground black
    pepper
2 tablespoons finely chopped
    parsley
1 tablespoon finely chopped basil

1. Bring a large pan of water with 1 teaspoon salt to a boil. Cook spaghetti (5-6 minutes if fresh, 10-12 minutes if dried).

2. Drain in a wide colander, then transfer to a large bowl.

3. While pasta is cooking, heat olive oil in a frying pan and add garlic. Fry lightly and season with salt and pepper.

4. Pour the garlic oil over the spaghetti, add parsley and basil, mix and serve at once.

VARIATION: For a mildly hot version, add a finely chopped chili pepper at stage 3.

PENNE IN MEAT AND SAGE SAUCE

penne al ragu

Penne are the short, hollow noodles.

INGREDIENTS:

1½ lbs. penne
½ cup olive oil
½ chopped garlic clove
1 onion, finely chopped
1 carrot, finely diced
2 oz. smoked beef, finely chopped
10 oz. ground veal
½ cup finely chopped parsley
10 fresh sage leaves
1 cup dry white wine
Salt and freshly ground black
pepper

1. Heat oil in a heavy saucepan, add garlic, onion and carrot, and sauté for about 10 minutes.

2. Add smoked beef and veal, and fry until lightly browned.

3. Add parsley, sage, and wine, season with salt and pepper to taste, and bring to a boil. Reduce heat to minimum, cover and cook for 1 hour. If necessary, add a little water during cooking.

4. Fill a large pan with water, add 1 teaspoon of salt and bring to a boil. Cook pasta for 8-10 minutes.

5. Drain the penne in a wide colander and then transfer to a heated bowl.

6. Pour sauce over penne, mix, and serve.

MACARONI IN MEAT SAUCE

ragu

INGREDIENTS:

1½ lbs. macaroni

SAUCE:

⅓ cup olive oil
1 chopped garlic clove
1 onion, finely chopped
2 celery stalks, thinly sliced
1 carrot, finely diced
10 oz. chopped beef
4 chopped chicken livers
8-10 dried porcini mushrooms,
soaked in warm water for at
least 20 minutes
½ cup dry white wine
1 cup water
1 bay leaf
Salt and freshly ground black
pepper
Grated nutmeg

1. Make the sauce: Heat olive oil in a heavy pot, add garlic, onion, celery and carrot and sauté for about 10 minutes. Stir every once in a while.

2. Add meat and chopped livers, and fry until browned. Add mushrooms and mix.

3. Add wine and water, bay leaf, salt, pepper, and nutmeg to taste and bring to a boil.

4. Reduce heat to minimum, cover, and cook for about an hour.

5. Fill a large pan with water, add 1 teaspoon of salt, and bring to a boil. Add macaroni and cook for about 10 minutes. Drain in a wide colander.

6. Transfer macaroni to a large heated bowl, carefully pour sauce on top, and mix well.

Spinach, ricotta and fresh tomatoes – that's all there is to it. Here, butter substitutes the olive oil.

RAVIOLI IN BUTTER AND FRESH TOMATO SAUCE

ravioli burro

<u>INGREDIENTS:</u>

1½ lbs. ravioli
3 oz. butter
Salt and freshly ground black
   pepper
Fresh tomato sauce (p. 92)
2 oz. finely grated Parmesan

1. Bring a large pan of water to the boil, and add 1 teaspoon salt. Add ravioli and cook for 8-10 minutes.

2. Drain in a wide colander and transfer to a large bowl.

3. Melt butter in a frying pan, pour on the ravioli and season with salt and pepper to taste.

4. Place a little of the tomato sauce in the center of each serving plate, surround with a few ravioli, sprinkle with garted Parmesan and serve at once.

Ewe's milk cheeses aging in a cellar.

MACARONI IN TOMATO AND PEPPER SAUCE

macaroni con pomodoro e peperoni

INGREDIENTS:

1½ lbs. macaroni

SAUCE:

6 ripe tomatoes
2 sweet red peppers
1 large onion, chopped
3 garlic cloves (whole)
½ cup olive oil
5 sprigs parsley
1 bay leaf
1 teaspoon oregano
10 fresh basil leaves
Salt and freshly ground black
    pepper to taste

1. Make the sauce: Scald tomatoes in boiling water, peel, and dice.

2. Clean peppers and cut into large squares.

3. Place all ingredients in a large pan, add ½ cup of water, and cook over a low heat for about 45 minutes. If necessary, add more water during cooking.

4. Discard parsley sprigs and press through a fine sieve. Return sieved sauce to saucepan and reheat.

5. Fill a large saucepan with water, add 1 teaspoon salt and bring to the boil. Add macaroni and cook for 8-10 minutes. Drain in a colander.

6. Transfer macaroni to a heated bowl, add sauce, and mix well. Serve with finely grated Parmesan.

LASAGNE

INGREDIENTS:

1 lb. lasagne leaves (either fresh or
    dried)
2 lbs. ripe tomatoes
3 chopped garlic cloves
½ cup quality olive oil
Salt and freshly ground black
    pepper
10 oz. mozzarella
3 oz. finely grated Parmesan
    cheese
10 fresh basil leaves, cut into thin
    strips

1. Scald tomatoes in boiling water and peel.

2. Place tomatoes, garlic, oil, salt and pepper in a food-processor fitted with a steel blade and work for a few seconds.

3. Slice mozzarella into ¼ inch thick slices.

4. Fill a large pan with water, add 1 teaspoon salt, and bring to a boil. Add lasagne strips and cook for a very short time (2-3 minutes for fresh dough, according to instructions on package if dried). Spread on a kitchen towel. Preheat oven to medium (350°F., 180°C.).

5. Grease the bottom of a rectangular oven-proof baking dish and cover with a few lasagne strips.

6. Arrange slices of mozzarella on dough, cover with a third of the sauce, and sprinkle some Parmesan and basil leaves on top.

7. Cover with an additional layer of dough strips and cover with mozzarella, sauce, Parmesan, and basil. Repeat to make three layers. Cover with a final layer of lasagne strips and brush with a little olive oil. Add another layer of cheese.

8. Bake in preheated oven for 30 minutes. Remove from oven, cut into servings and serve hot.

CANNELLONI

INGREDIENTS:

12 6×6 inch squares fresh pasta
  dough
1 lb. ricotta
2 egg yolks
3 oz. finely grated Parmesan
3 oz. softened butter
Salt and freshly ground black
  pepper
A pinch of grated nutmeg
A few fresh rosemary sprigs

1. Make the filling: Place ricotta,
egg yolks, Parmesan and
1½ oz. butter in a bowl. Mix well
and season with salt, pepper and
nutmeg. Chill.

2. Bring a large pan of water to the
boil and add 1 teaspoon salt. Add
dough squares and cook for
2-3 minutes. Remove and spread
on a kitchen towel to drain.

3. Place a row of the ricotta
mixture along the center of a
square, and fold the dough from
both sides to cover filling. Fill all the
squares in this manner. Preheat
oven to medium (350° F., 180° C.).

4. Arrange the stuffed canneloni in
a large, oven-proof baking dish, dot
with remaining butter and garnish
with rosemary.

5. Bake in preheated oven for
15-20 minutes and serve hot.

VARIATION: Cook 8 oz. fresh
spinach leaves for 3 minutes in
boiling salted water, chop coarsely
and add to filling.

PASTA SHELLS WITH EGGPLANTS AND TOMATOES

conchisili con melanzane e pomodoro

INGREDIENTS:

1½ lbs. shell pasta

SAUCE:

½ cup olive oil
2 chopped garlic cloves
1 chopped onion
6 tomatoes, scalded, peeled and
  chopped
Salt and freshly ground black
  pepper
1 eggplant, cut into 1 inch cubes
2 tablespoons chopped fresh basil

1. Make the sauce: Heat olive oil in
a small pan, add garlic and onion,
and saute for 10 minutes. Add
tomatoes and season with salt and
pepper. Reduce heat to minimum
and cook, covered, for about
30 minutes.

2. In another frying pan, deep-fry
eggplant cubes until well browned.
Remove with a slotted spoon and
add to tomato sauce. Stir, add basil
and remove from heat.

3. Bring a large pan of water to the
boil and add 1 teaspoon salt. Add
pasta and cook until done. Drain
well in a large colander and transfer
to a large bowl.

4. Pour sauce on pasta and mix
carefully. Serve with finely grated
Parmesan.

SPAGHETTI IN FRESH TOMATO SAUCE

spaghetti al pomodoro

INGREDIENTS:

1½ lbs. spaghetti

SAUCE:

6 ripe tomatoes
½ cup olive oil
1 chopped garlic clove
2 tablespoons finely chopped
fresh basil leaves
Salt and freshly ground black
pepper
Fresh basil leaves, to garnish

1. Make the sauce: Scald tomatoes in boiling water and peel.

2. Place tomatoes in food-processor fitted with a steel blade and work to a smooth puree.

3. Transfer to a bowl. Add garlic, basil and oil, season with salt and pepper to taste and stir well. Cover and set aside, to allow flavors to blend.

4. Fill a large pan with water, add 1 tablespoon salt and bring to a boil. Add spaghetti and cook until done (5-6 minutes if fresh, 10-12 minutes if dried). Drain in a large colander.

5. Remove the spaghetti to individual plates, ladle a generous amount of sauce on each, garnish with basil leaves, and serve.

STRAW AND HAY

paglia e fieno

The different colored pastas, mixed on the same plate, give this dish its name.

INGREDIENTS:

11 oz. plain fettuccine
11 oz. green (spinach) fettuccine
2½ oz. butter
Salt and freshly ground black
  pepper
3 oz. finely grated Parmesan

1. Bring a large pan of water to the boil and add 1 teaspoon salt. Add both kinds of fettuccine and cook until done (3-5 minutes if fresh, 8-10 minutes if dried).

2. Drain in a large colander and transfer to a large heated bowl.

3. Melt butter gently in a small pan, season with salt and pepper.

4. Pour the melted butter over fettuccine, add Parmesan cheese, and mix well.

5. Serve at once.

Half a cup fresh or frozen peas may be added in stage 3.

The library of an old house in Tuscany. The owner himself fills the Chianti bottles from a large barrel.

FETTUCCINE ALFREDO

INGREDIENTS:

1½ lbs. fettuccine

SAUCE:

1 cup cream
4 tablespoons finely grated
    Parmesan cheese
Grated nutmeg
Salt and freshly ground black
    pepper
3 oz. softened butter

1. Make the sauce: Place cream in a saucepan and bring to a boil. Reduce heat and cook for 3-4 minutes, or until thickened a little. Lower heat, add cheese and nutmeg, season with salt and pepper to taste, and stir. Stir in the softened butter. Allow the butter to melt completely, making sure the sauce does not boil.

2. Fill a large pan with water, add 1 teaspoon salt and bring to a boil. Add fettuccine and cook until done (3 4 minutes if fresh, 7-10 minutes if dried). Drain in a large colander.

3. Transfer fettuccine to a large bowl. Add sauce, mix well, and serve.

FETTUCCINE WITH ZUCCHINI

INGREDIENTS:

1½ lbs. fettuccine
6 small, firm zucchini (courgettes)
½ cup quality olive oil
2 chopped garlic cloves
Salt and freshly ground black
    pepper
3 oz. Parmesan cheese, finely
    grated

1. Slice the zucchini very thinly, without peeling.

2. Heat oil in a large frying pan, add garlic and sauté for a few minutes.

3. Add zucchini, sauté for a further 3-4 minutes, stirring occasionally. Season with salt and pepper.

4. Fill a large pan with water, bring to the boil and add 1 teaspoon of salt. Add fettuccine and cook until done (3-4 minutes if fresh, 7-10 minutes if dried). Drain in a large colander.

5. Transfer fettuccine to a large bowl. Carefully pour fried zucchini and oil on top of fettuccine and mix well. Add grated cheese and serve.

PASTA IN MUSHROOM SAUCE

pasta in salsa funghi

INGREDIENTS:

1½ lbs. spaghetti or fettuccine
1 pkg. dried porcini mushrooms,
    soaked in warm water for at
    least 20 minutes
2 oz. butter
10 oz. fresh champignons, thinly
    sliced
1 cup cream
Salt and freshly ground black
    pepper
1 tablespoon chopped parsley
4 tablespoons finely grated
    Parmesan (optional)

1. Squeeze the water from the soaked dried mushrooms.

2. Melt butter in a frying pan. When the butter begins to sizzle, add both the sliced fresh and dried mushrooms, and sauté for about 5 minutes.

3. Add cream, season with salt and pepper, bring to a boil, and cook for another 4-5 minutes.

4. Bring a large pan of water to the boil and add 1 teaspoon of salt. Add pasta and cook until done (3-5 minutes if fresh, 8-10 minutes if dried). Drain and transfer to a large serving bowl.

5. Pour the mushroom sauce over the pasta, mix well, garnish with parsley, and serve.

Grated Parmesan may be added before serving.

FETTUCCINE WITH SARDINES

INGREDIENTS:

1½ lbs. broad fettuccine
12 fresh sardines, cleaned
½ cup quality olive oil
2 oz. pine nuts
2 chopped garlic cloves
1 green hot pepper, chopped
1 large onion, chopped
10 mushrooms, thickly sliced
2 sprigs of dill, chopped
Salt and freshly ground black
    pepper

1. Heat ¼ cup oil in a frying pan, add the sardines and fry for 2 minutes. Remove from pan and set aside. Add pine nuts and fry until golden. Remove with a slotted spoon.

2. Add the remaining oil to the pan, add the garlic, pepper, and onion and sauté until the onion becomes transparent.

3. Add mushrooms and dill and sauté for another minute.

4. Return the sardines to the pan, season with salt and pepper, and mix the ingredients carefully. Keep the pan warm.

5. Fill a large pan with water, add 1 teaspoon salt, and bring to a boil. Add fettuccine and cook until done (3-5 minutes if fresh, 8-10 minutes if dried).

6. Drain in a large colander and divide the pasta among warmed individual serving bowls.

7. Top each bowl with sardines and vegetables. Garnish with fried pine nuts and serve at once.

Wide fettucine, fresh fish, lots of hot peppers – pasta Southern-style.

POLENTA BASIC RECIPE

INGREDIENTS:

1 lb. corn meal
Salt and freshly ground black
pepper
3 oz. butter, melted
2 oz. grated Parmesan

1. Bring 3 cups of water to a boil in a large pan. Add 2 teaspoons salt. Add corn meal and stir well, blending the corn meal into the water completely. Reduce heat and cook, stirring constantly with a wooden spoon, until the polenta is thick and separates from sides of pan. If necessary, add a little water during cooking.

2. Add melted butter and Parmesan, stir, and serve hot.

FRIED POLENTA

polenta fritta

1. Prepare the basic polenta recipe.

2. Thoroughly grease a rectangular baking pan with olive oil. Spoon cooked polenta into the pan and spread evenly. Smooth surface with an oiled spatula. Chill for an hour.

3. Turn the polenta out on to a cutting board. Heat olive oil in a frying pan. Cut the polenta into 2 inch squares, dip in flour and fry on both sides until brown and crisp. Serve with grated Parmesan cheese or fresh tomato sauce (p. 92).

BAKED POLENTA

polenta al forno

INGREDIENTS:

1 lb. corn meal
Tomato and sweet pepper sauce
(p. 88)
3 oz. finely grated Parmesan

1. Prepare the basic polenta recipe.

2. Spoon the cooked polenta into a large, well greased baking pan. Smooth to an even layer about $1/2$ inch thick and chill for an hour.

3. Cut out circles, using a glass or a cooky-cutter.

4. Arrange circles in an oval oven-proof baking pan in overlapping rows. Preheat oven to medium-high (400° F., 200° C.).

5. Cover polenta with a layer of tomato and sweet pepper sauce, then top with grated Parmesan.

6. Bake in preheated oven for about 20 minutes. Serve at once.

VEGETABLE RISOTTO

risoto con verdure

INGREDIENTS:

½ cup quality olive oil
1 fresh, firm leek, thinly sliced
1 carrot, diced
2 celery stalks, thinly sliced
1 cup green peas
2 tomatoes, scalded, peeled and
  chopped
½ chopped cup parsley
Salt and freshly ground black
  pepper
2½ oz. butter
1 onion, finely chopped
1 lb. arboria rice
1 cup dry white wine
5 cups water
3 oz. finely grated Parmesan

1. Prepare the vegetables: Heat 1 cup olive oil in a frying pan, add the leek, carrot and celery and sauté for about 10 minutes. Add peas, tomatoes and parsley, season with salt and pepper to taste and sauté for a few more minutes.

2. Place ¼ cup olive oil and 1 oz. butter in a large fire-proof casserole, add onion and saute. Add rice and stir well.

3. Add wine and 1 cup water, bring to a boil, reduce heat and cook until most of the liquids have been absorbed. Stir occasionally. Add more water and continue cooking until all liquids have been absorbed.

4. Add vegetables and mix well.

5. Add remaining butter and the Parmesan, correct seasoning if necessary, stir and serve.

SAFFRON RISOTTO

risotto alla milanese

Risotto is a moist, juicy, tasty rice dish, the classic Italian method to cook rice.

INGREDIENTS:

1 lb. rice
1 onion, finely chopped
3 oz. butter
1 cup dry white wine
1 teaspoon saffron strands
3 oz. finely grated Parmesan
Salt and freshly ground black
  pepper
5 cups boiling water

1. Heat 1½ oz. butter in a large saucepan, add onion and sauté for about 10 minutes.

2. Add rice and sauté for 2-3 minutes. Add saffron, wine and 1 cup of the boiling water. Reduce heat to a minimum.

3. Cook, stirring frequently, until most of the liquid has been absorbed, and add another cup of the water. Continue adding water until rice is al dente.

4. Stir in remaining butter and the grated Parmesan and serve at once.

VEGETABLES

Vegetables play an important role in the Italian cuisine. They are chosen with careful attention to their freshness and quality. It is a mistake to assume that if tomatoes are to be pureed, thay can be of inferior quality. When choosing vegetables, select them with care and buy only the best and freshest, in season. Do not insist on vegetables out of season. Their time will come, too.

A journey through Italy's markets is a delightful experience of colors, fragrances and tastes. Italy has been blessed with an enviable variety of leafy vegetables, such as various kinds of lettuce – green, red, bitter, sweet, large and small. When separated into leaves and mixed in a large bowl, with olive oil and wine vinegar, they serve as a marvelously refreshing course after a heavy beef stew or a large, juicy steak.

In season, red tomatoes are sold still attached to sprigs from the bush. They bring back memories of "days gone by", of tomatoes untouched by hormone experts who give us tomatoes all year round, but robbed them of their flavor.
The stalls are piled with wild mushrooms, the most famous of which are the porcini, available only dried; and the Italian truffles.

If you manage to get truffles, rinse them clean of sand and grate them coarsely onto pasta in butter, cream, or olive oil sauce. They can also be sliced thickly and added to meat or vegetable dishes.

In an Italian meal, vegetables may be served as dishes on their own, as part of other dishes, while others become side dishes, accompanying the main course. These may include thin, crisp beans; firm broccoli flowers, marinated or cooked in sauce; cooked or steamed white beans; small artichokes, and many more. Most are flavored with fine olive oil, wine vinegar, garlic and herbs.

Vegetables also come in another form – cooked salads made of zucchini, eggplants, sweet red and green peppers, and fleshy beetroots. These can be made in a large quantity and will keep for a few days.

Stuffed vegetables can be the main course in a light, simple meal – onions, zucchini, eggplants, and peppers, stuffed with a rich variety of meat, cheese, and herb fillings. They are mostly baked, and vegetable and filling receive equal attention.

The zucchini, so often colourless and boring, is picked young, small and fresh, dipped in thin batter and deep-fried. Thence it emerges golden, crisp and hot, soft and tasty inside to be served immediately.

.Vegetables play a star role in the making of antipasti, sauces, and mixed dishes. They join forces with pasta, meat, and cheeses, to accompany virtually every Italian meal.

GREEN SALAD

insalata verde

INGREDIENTS:

Several varieties of lettuce
Extra virgin olive oil
Wine vinegar
Salt and freshly ground black
  pepper

1. Use several varieties of lettuce: cabbage lettuce, red lettuce, Cos lettuce, chicory and rucolo lettuce. The leaves should be young and firm, as fresh as possible.

2. Separate into leaves. Tear into small pieces. Rinse and dry thoroughly (this is very important!)

3. Place leaves in a large bowl. Pour a generous measure of olive oil and 1/4 the amount wine vinegar. Season with salt and pepper to taste, mix well and serve at once.

This refreshing salad is ideally served following a heavy main course.

FRIED EGGPLANT

melanzane fritte

INGREDIENTS:

2 firm, fresh eggplants
1 tablespoon salt
½ cup olive oil
Salt and freshly ground black
   pepper
Juice of 1 lemon
2 tablespoons chopped parsley

1. Slice eggplants into lengthwise
strips, sprinkle with salt and set
aside for 20 minutes. Rinse and
wipe dry.

2. Heat olive oil in a frying pan, add
eggplant slices, a few at a time,
and fry until golden.

3. Arrange eggplant slices on a
serving dish and season with salt
and pepper. Sprinkle with a little
olive oil and lemon juice, and
garnish with parsley.

BAKED EGGPLANTS WITH TOMATOES AND CHEESE

melanzane al forno

INGREDIENTS:

3 small, firm, fresh eggplants
1 tablespoon salt
½ cup + 2 tablespoons olive oil
2 chopped garlic cloves
1 lb. tomatoes, scalded, peeled and
*   chopped*
Salt and freshly ground black
*   pepper*
20 chopped basil or mint leaves
½ lb. crumbled mozzarella
4 tablespoons finely grated
*   Parmesan*

1. Slice eggplants crosswise into ½ inch slices, sprinkle with salt and set aside for 20 minutes. Rinse and wipe dry.

2. Heat ½ cup olive oil in a frying pan, add eggplant slices and fry until golden. Drain on kitchen paper. Pour off oil from frying pan and wipe with paper towels. Preheat oven to medium (350° F., 180° C.).

3. Heat the remaining tablespoons of olive oil in the frying pan, add garlic, and fry until browned. Add tomatoes and basil or mint, and season with salt and pepper. Stir and cook, covered, for about 15 minutes.

4. Arrange eggplant slices in a baking pan, top with a layer of tomato sauce and sprinkle both cheeses on top. Bake for about 30 minutes.

FRIED EGGPLANT AND MOZZARELLA "SANDWICHES"

"panini" di melanzane e mozzarella

INGREDIENTS:

2 small, elongated eggplants
7 oz. mozzarella or goats' cheese
Salt and freshly ground black
*   pepper*
12 basil leaves
1 cup plain white flour
2 eggs, beaten
Oil for deep frying

1. Slice eggplants crosswise in ³/₄ inch thick slices. Slice each again almost all the way through, forming a sandwich, but leave the slice attached at the bottom.

2. Slice cheese and season with salt and pepper.

3. Stuff each eggplant "sandwich" with a slice of cheese and a basil leaf.

4. Secure the sandwich with a toothpick, dip each in flour, then egg, and flour again. Heat oil for deep frying and fry eggplants on both sides until well browned. Drain on kitchen paper and serve at once.

FRIED ZUCCHINI

zucchine fritti

INGREDIENTS:

12 small, firm zucchini

BATTER:

1 cup plain flour
Salt and freshly ground black
_   pepper_
1 egg
2 tablespoons olive oil
Approximately ½ cup cold water
Oil for deep frying
3 lemons, quartered

1. Prepare batter: Place flour in a bowl and season with salt and pepper. Add egg and olive oil and stir. Gradually add water, beating continuously, to make a smooth batter. If batter seems too thick, add a little more water.

2. Halve zucchini crosswise, then quarter halves lengthwise.

3. Immerse the zucchini in batter and stir well.

4. Heat oil for deep frying. Remove zucchini one by one from the batter and fry until crisp and golden.

5. Drain on kitchen towels, transfer to a serving dish, and serve at once, with quartered lemons.

STUFFED ZUCCHINI

zucchine ripieni

INGREDIENTS:

12 very small zucchini
½ cup breadcrumbs
A handful of mint leaves, chopped
A large bunch of parsley, finely
*   chopped*
3 tablespoons grated Parmesan
4 finely chopped garlic cloves
Salt and freshly ground black
*   pepper*
½ cup fine olive oil

1. Preheat oven to medium
(350° F., 180° C.). Cut zucchini in
half lengthwise and spoon out pulp,
to make hollow boat-like shells.

2. Chop the pulp and mix with
breadcrumbs, mint, parsley,
Parmesan, garlic and olive oil.
Season with salt and pepper. Fill
zucchini shells with mixture.

3. Grease an oven-proof dish with
olive oil and arrange stuffed
zucchini in it. Pour a little water at
bottom of dish. Bake for about
30 minutes.

*The fountain in Piazza del
Campo in Siena.*

ZUCCHINI WITH
PARMESAN AND SAGE

zucchini parmigiano e salvia

INGREDIENTS:

12 very small zucchini
Salt and freshly ground black
*   pepper*
3 oz. finely grated Parmesan
2 oz. butter
1 tablespoon chopped sage leaves

1. Wash zucchini, but do not peel.
Cook them in boiling water for
about 5 minutes, allow to cool and
slice diagonally to ½ inch thick
slices.

2. Place slices in a large bowl,
season with salt and pepper and
sprinkle with Parmesan.

3. Melt butter in a frying pan, add
sage leaves and fry until butter
begins to brown. Pour boiling butter
on zucchini, stir and serve at once.

FRESH GREEN BEANS IN TOMATO SAUCE

fagiolini al pomodoro

INGREDIENTS:

1½ lbs. very fresh, very thin green
  beans
⅓ cup olive oil
1 chopped garlic clove
1 small onion, chopped
6 ripe tomatoes, scalded, peeled,
  and chopped
Salt and freshly ground black
  pepper

1. Wash beans, snip off edges and
cook in boiling salted water for
5 minutes. Drain and rinse under
running cold water.

2. Heat olive oil in a saucepan, add
garlic and onion and fry for about
5 minutes.

3. Add tomatoes, season with salt
and pepper and cook for another
5 minutes. Add ½ cup water, stir
and add beans. Stir, reduce heat
and cook, covered, for about
20 minutes.

*Lucca, from the top of the
bell-fry. The beans were
cooked in the best restaurant
in town, "Buca Antonio."*

Half a dozen leafy greens for the salad.

SWISS CHARD WITH ANCHOVIES

bietole con acciughe

INGREDIENTS:

2 lbs. Swiss chard
3 tablespoons olive oil
4 chopped garlic cloves
6 anchovy fillets, chopped
Salt and freshly ground black
  pepper

1. Rinse Swiss chard carefully and chop leaves into 2 inch pieces. Cook in boiling salted water for 2 minutes. Drain, and squeeze out excess moisture.

2. Heat olive oil in a large frying pan, add garlic and anchovy, and fry for 2 minutes.

3. Add Swiss chard, season to taste, stir, reduce heat and cook, covered, for about 5 minutes. Serve hot.

BROCCOLI IN OLIVE OIL AND GARLIC

INGREDIENTS:

1¼ lbs. fresh broccoli
4 garlic cloves, thinly sliced
½ cup quality olive oil
Salt and freshly ground black
  pepper

1. Separate broccoli into flowerets, peel stalks and slice diagonally into ½ inch pieces. Steam for 5 minutes. Transfer to a bowl.

2. Place olive oil and sliced garlic cloves in a small saucepan and heat slightly. Pour on broccoli, season with salt and pepper and stir.

This dish can be served lukewarm or cold.

PUREE OF WHITE BEANS WITH SPINACH

INGREDIENTS:

1 cup dried haricot beans, soaked overnight
2 celery stalks, thinly sliced
1 potato, peeled and diced
1 large onion, chopped
Salt and freshly ground black pepper
1/3 cup olive oil
2 lbs. spinach or Swiss chard, washed and coarsely chopped

1. Drain the soaked beans and place in a saucepan with celery, potato and onion. Add water to cover and bring to a boil. Reduce heat and cook for about 1 1/2 hours, until very tender, almost mushy.

2. Transfer contents of pan to a food-processor fitted with a steel blade, season with salt and pepper, and work to a smooth puree. Gradually add olive oil while processor still working.

3. Cook spinach or Swiss chard in boiling salted water for about 3 minutes. Drain and squeeze dry.

4. Pile the bean puree on a large serving dish, surround it with spinach, dribble olive oil on both, and serve.

FENNEL WITH CHEESE

fenocchio con parmigiano

INGREDIENTS:

6 firm young fennel bulbs
2 oz. butter
1/4 cup milk or cream
Salt and freshly ground black pepper
Grated nutmeg
4 tablespoons grated Parmesan

1. Remove stalks and dried outer leaves from fennel bulbs. Using a sharp knife, cut each bulb lengthwise into 6 pieces. Preheat oven to high (425° F., 220° C.).

2. Cook fennel in gently boiling salted water for 5-6 minutes. Drain.

3. Arrange fennels in an oven-proof dish, add butter and milk and season with salt, pepper, and nutmeg to taste. Sprinkle with grated cheese and bake for about 10 minutes. Serve at once.

VEGETABLE SALAD

insalata verdure

INGREDIENTS:

2 potatoes
2 carrots, peeled
1/2 lb. fresh green beans, sliced into 1/2 inch pieces
2 small zucchini
2 firm young beetroots, peeled
1/2 cup quality olive oil
1/3 cup wine vinegar
Salt and freshly ground black pepper
20 basil leaves, cut into thin strips

1. Cook potatoes until tender, allow to cool and peel; cook carrots for 7-8 minutes and allow to cool; cook beans for about 3 minutes and allow to cool; cook zucchini for about 3 minutes and allow to cool; cook beetroots in a little water for about 15 minutes, reserve cooking liquids. Allow to cool.

2. Cut all vegetables into 1/2 inch cubes. Place in a bowl.

3. Mix oil, vinegar, 1/2 a cup of reserved beetroot water in a separate bowl. Season with salt and pepper and add basil. Pour over vegetables and chill for a few hours before serving.

PUREE OF LEEKS BAKED IN ZUCCHINI SAUCE

soffito pori in salsa zucchini

INGREDIENTS:

2 lbs. leeks
7 oz. ricotta
3 oz. grated Parmesan
3 eggs
4 tablespoons quality olive oil
Salt and freshly ground black
    pepper

SAUCE:

4 tablespoons olive oil
2 chopped garlic cloves
1 small onion, chopped
1 carrot, diced
1 celery stalk, thinly sliced
1 lb. small zucchini, thinly sliced
2 ripe tomatoes, scalded, peeled
    and chopped
3/4 cup dry white wine
1 tablespoon marjoram
1 tablespoon oregano
Salt and freshly ground black
    pepper

1. Discard the root end and most of the green part of the leeks. Clean thoroughly. Cut into 2 inch pieces and cook in boiling salted water for about 40 minutes. Drain, rinse under running water and squeeze well. Preheat oven to medium (350° F., 180° C.).

2. Puree the leek, with both cheeses, the eggs, and the olive oil in a food-processor fitted with a steel blade. Season with salt and pepper, and work to a smooth puree.

3. Grease a heat-proof rectangular baking pan with a little olive oil. Pour the puree into the pan, smooth to an even layer and bake for about 45 minutes. If top browns too quickly, cover with foil.

4. While the leeks are baking, prepare the sauce: Heat olive oil in a frying pan, add garlic, carrot and celery and fry for 5 minutes; add zucchini and fry a further 3 minutes; add tomatoes and stir. Add wine, marjoram, and oregano, season with salt and pepper and cook for 20 minutes. Allow to cool slightly, transfer to a food-processor and work to a very smooth puree.

5. To serve, pour a serving of the sauce on a flat plate, and place a 2½ inch square of the baked leeks in the center of the plate.

Both the leeks and the sauce should be served warm or at room temperature, rather than hot.

POTATOES BAKED WITH MILK

patate al latte

INGREDIENTS:

2 lbs. potatoes, peeled
3 cups milk
1 tablespoon butter
2 chopped garlic cloves
Salt and freshly ground black
  pepper
Grated nutmeg
6 basil leaves, finely chopped
3 tablespoons finely grated
  Parmesan

1. Slice potatoes into $\frac{1}{4}$-$\frac{1}{2}$ inch slices.

2. Place milk in a saucepan and bring to a boil. Add potatoes, reduce heat and cook until just tender. Drain.

3. Preheat oven to medium-high (400 F., 200 C.). Butter a heat-proof baking dish and layer the potato slices. Pour over about $\frac{1}{2}$ cup of the milk in which potatoes have been cooked, and sprinkle with garlic, salt, pepper, nutmeg, basil and Parmesan.

4. Bake in preheated oven for 10-15 minutes and serve at once.

POTATOES WITH ANCHOVIES AND OLIVES

INGREDIENTS:

2 lbs. large potatoes, peeled
$\frac{1}{3}$ cup quality olive oil
3 oz. black olives, pitted and
  coarsely chopped
2 tablespoons capers, coarsely
  chopped
4 anchovy fillets, coarsely chopped
A pinch of salt and freshly ground
  black pepper
2 tablespoons chopped parsley

1. Quarter the potatoes, and then slice into 1 inch slices.

2. Heat oil in a large frying pan, add potatoes, olives, capers, and anchovies. Season with salt and pepper, and stir.

3. Reduce heat to a minimum and cook, covered, for about 30 minutes. Stir carefully every once in a while.

4. Transfer to a serving dish, sprinkle with parsley, and serve.

ARTICHOKES JEWISH STYLE

carciofi alla giudea

A popular dish, simple and tasty.

INGREDIENTS:

6 small, young artichokes
$\frac{1}{2}$ a lemon
Oil for deep frying

1. Discard outer leaves, cut off upper half of artichokes and trim stalk to within 2 inches from base. Scoop out the fuzzy choke from inside and rub cut surfaces with half a lemon.

2. Pour enough oil into a deep frying pan to cover artichokes (about $1\frac{1}{2}$-2 inches) and heat. When sizzling, add artichokes, cut side down. Fry, pressing artichokes to the bottom of the pan.

The artichokes open out like a flower and the leaves become crisp and tasty. Fry for 7-8 minutes, until leaves are golden. Serve hot.

GLAZED TURNIPS

INGREDIENTS:

2 lbs. turnips
2 tablespoons butter
Salt and freshly ground black
  pepper
1 whole clove
2 tablespoons sugar

1. Peel turnips and slice into $\frac{1}{4}$ inch slices.

2. Place turnip slices and butter in a saucepan, season with salt and pepper, and add the clove and $\frac{1}{4}$ cup water. Cover and cook on a medium-low heat until all liquids have evaporated and the turnips are just tender. Stir occasionally.

3. Add sugar and cook a further 2 minutes, stirring carefully. Serve hot.

TOMATOES WITH MARJORAM FILLING

pomodore ripieno

INGREDIENTS:

6 large, ripe tomatoes
1/2 cup quality olive oil
3 tablespoons chopped fresh
　marjoram
3 chopped garlic cloves
4 tablespoons breadcrumbs
Salt and freshly ground black
　pepper

1. Preheat oven to medium
(350° F., 180° C.). Slice about 1/4
inch off the top of each tomato,
and, using a spoon, scoop out the
pulp and seeds. Turn upside down
to rest.

2. In a bowl, mix half the olive oil
with the marjoram, garlic, and
breadcrumbs. Season with salt and
pepper, and spoon the stuffing into
the hollowed tomatoes.

3. Arrange stuffed tomatoes in a
heat-proof dish, sprinkle with
remaining olive oil and bake for
30 minutes. Serve hot.

VEGETABLE STEW

INGREDIENTS:

3 artichokes
1 lemon, halved
1/2 lb. scallions, cut into 2 inch
　pieces
1 cup fresh green peas
1 cup fresh green beans
1/3 cup olive oil
Salt and freshly ground black
　pepper
1/2 cup dry white wine
Juice of 1/2 a lemon
Small bunch parsley, coarsely
　chopped

1. Cut off and discard outer leaves
of artichokes. Slice off top two
thirds of artichokes and discard.
Rub cut surface with half a lemon
to prevent discoloring; quarter
artichokes lengthwise, cut out
fuzzy inner choke and again rub
cut surfaces with half a lemon.

2. Place oil and vegetables in a
large pan, season with salt and
pepper, and cook, stirring
occasionally, for about 10 minutes.
Add wine, reduce heat to minimum
and cook, covered, for about
30 minutes. Add a little water if
necessary.

3. Taste and correct seasoning.
Add lemon juice and parsley, stir,
and serve.

RED CABBAGE BRAISED IN WINE

INGREDIENTS:

1 red cabbage
3 tablespoons butter
1 cup dry red wine
1 tablespoon sugar
¼ cup wine vinegar
Salt and freshly ground black
  pepper

1. Cut cabbage in half lengthwise, and slice each half into thin strips, removing core.

2. Heat butter in a large saucepan, add cabbage strips and stir gently until they are thoroughly coated with butter.

3. Add the red wine and sugar, season with salt and pepper, and bring to a boil. Reduce heat and cook, covered, for about 30 minutes.

4. Add vinegar, stir, cover and cook another 15 minutes.

SPINACH WITH RAISINS AND PINE NUTS

spinaci con uvetta e pignoli

INGREDIENTS:

18 slices French bread, ½ inch
  thick
A little olive oil
2 lbs. fresh spinach, washed,
  cleaned and coarsely chopped
⅓ cup olive oil
2 garlic cloves, finely chopped
3 oz. pine nuts
2 tablespoons raisins, soaked in
  water
Salt and freshly ground black
  pepper

1. Rub bread with olive oil and toast for a few minutes.

2. Steam spinach for 2-3 minutes. Transfer to a serving bowl.

3. Heat olive oil in a frying pan, add garlic and fry for one minute. Add pine nuts and fry until golden. Add raisins, season with salt and pepper, mix and remove from heat.

4. Pour contents of frying pan over the spinach. Stir and serve at once, with toasted bread.

STUFFED ONIONS

cipolle ripieni

INGREDIENTS:

6 medium onions, unpeeled

FILLING:

6 anchovy fillets, finely chopped
1/2 cup chopped parsley
3 chopped garlic cloves
1/2 cup breadcrumbs
Salt and freshly ground black
  pepper
1/2 cup olive oil

1. Drop unpeeled onions in boiling water and cook for about 15 minutes. Remove, drain, and rinse under running water. Peel.

2. Cut each onion in half lengthwise. Using a spoon, remove inner layers to make 12 hollow boat-like shells.

3. Mix remaining ingredients for the stuffing, and fill the onions. Preheat an oven to medium (350° F., 180° C.).

4. Grease an ovenproof dish with some olive oil, arrange stuffed onions in it, sprinkle with a little olive oil and bake in for 45-50 minutes. Serve very hot.

MUSHROOMS IN LEMON

funghi con limone

INGREDIENTS:

1 lb. fresh, firm mushrooms
1 1/2 oz. butter
2 chopped garlic cloves
Salt and freshly ground black
  pepper
2 tablespoons chopped parsley
Juice of 1/2 a lemon

1. Clean and slice mushrooms.

2. Melt butter in a frying pan, add garlic and fry for 1 minute. Add mushrooms and fry for 4-5 minutes. Season with salt and pepper.

3. Add parsley and stir. Add lemon juice, cook for an additional minute, and serve.

STUFFED PEPPERS

peperoni ripieni

<u>INGREDIENTS:</u>

6 fresh sweet peppers (red, yellow
  or green)
1½ lbs. lean beef, diced finely
1 onion, chopped
2 chopped garlic cloves
2 oz. margarine
7 oz. button mushrooms, quartered
Salt and freshly ground black
  pepper
⅓ cup dry white wine
A little olive oil

1. Slice about 1 inch off the stem
end of each pepper and reserve.
Carefully remove the seeds from
the peppers.

2. Heat margarine in a frying pan,
add garlic and onion, and sauté.
Add veal and mushrooms and cook
for 3 minutes. Season with salt and
pepper, add wine and cook for
about 5 more minutes. Remove
from heat and allow to cool.
Preheat oven to medium
(350° F., 180° C.).

3. Brush the peppers (inside and
out) with olive oil. Bake, empty, in
preheated oven for about
20 minutes, with the "caps" on.

4. Stuff peppers with meat mixture,
cover with "caps" and bake an
additional 30 minutes. Serve hot.

One must bear in mind that Italy is almost totally surrounded by water, lots of water. This means plenty of shellfish and fish dishes. Italy has two kinds of markets: the vegetable and fruit markets in every town and village; and the fish markets in all the coastal settlements. Those are many.

An Italian fish market is a true delight for sea-food enthusiasts. To see it in full regalia, one must rise very early. The Rialto fish market in Venice, at four o'clock in the morning, can be an unforgettable experience: The boats glide in slowly in the amazing light of this enchanted hour, and unload crate upon crate of the night's catch, an enormous variety of fish of all kinds, shapes and colors; crates of mussels, crabs, shrimp and squid, freshly caught and fragrant with their characteristic smell.

Most of the catch will be eaten that very day, as fresh as possible, cooked as lightly as possible. The cooking will be simple and minimal, the fish lightly fried or grilled, so as not to destroy their flavor, freshness and texture.

The markets in the south, such as in Folia, are no less colorful and rich than the markets of the more aristocratic north. Those fish that can be eaten raw are eaten immediately, soon after they have been caught. The rest make rich and thick fish soups. Several kinds of fish and shellfish, lots of garlic, olive oil, tomatoes and herbs are all cooked in one pot. These soups are a whole meal, eaten slowly with a spoon, and with your fingers.

Many kinds of pasta dishes use fish. The taste varies in the different regions: hotter and spicier in the south, more delicate and refined in the north.

When preparing fish, adhere to the basic rules, applicable anywhere in the world: make sure your fish is fresh, and never overcook it.

BAKED SEA BREAM

INGREDIENTS:

6 fresh sea bream
Salt and freshly ground black
  pepper
1½ oz. butter
1 onion, finely chopped
2 carrots, diced
2 celery stalks, thinly sliced
2 chopped garlic cloves
1 cup dry white wine
1 tablespoon thyme
2 tablespoons chopped parsley

1. Preheat oven to medium-high (400°F., 200°C.). Season fish with salt and pepper.

2. Generously butter a roasting pan large enough to hold all the fish, using half the butter. Sprinkle the chopped vegetables and garlic over the bottom of the pan.

3. Arrange fish on top of vegetables, dot them with the remaining butter, dribble over the wine, and sprinkle with thyme.

4. Bake, uncovered, for about 20 minutes, occasionally basting fish with liquids accumulating in the bottom of the pan (add a little wine during baking, if necessary).

5. Remove the fish to a serving dish, top with some of the sauce and vegetables, and sprinkle with chopped parsley.

RED MULLET WITH MINT AND WHITE WINE

triglie nel vino bianco, con menthe

INGREDIENTS:

12 fresh red mullet, cleaned
Salt and freshly ground black
  pepper
24 mint leaves
6 garlic cloves, peeled and halved
  lengthwise
½ cup flour
⅓ cup olive oil

1. Season the fish with salt and pepper. Stuff 2 mint leaves and ½ a garlic clove into the cavity of each fish.

2. Roll the fish in flour and shake to remove excess. Fry fish in the oil for 2 minutes on each side. Remove from pan and keep hot. Wipe pan clean.

3. Prepare the sauce: Heat the olive oil in the frying pan, add the onion and sauté until soft. Add the wine, vinegar, and parsley, and season with salt and pepper. Bring to a boil and cook until reduced to half.

4. Arrange fish on a serving dish and pour over the sauce. Garnish with mint leaves.

RED MULLET IN TOMATO SAUCE

triglie alla livornese

INGREDIENTS:

12 fresh red mullet
Salt and freshly ground black
  pepper
1/2 cup quality olive oil
3 chopped garlic cloves
1 fresh hot chili pepper, chopped
2 lbs. ripe tomatoes, scalded,
  peeled and finely chopped
10 leaves basil, finely chopped
1 cup dry white wine
1 tablespoon finely chopped
  parsley

1. Season fish with salt and pepper. Heat olive oil in a large frying pan. When very hot, add fish and fry for about 2 minutes on each side. Remove and set aside.

2. Add garlic and hot pepper to the pan and fry for 2 minutes. Add tomatoes, basil, and wine, season with salt and pepper, and bring to a boil. Reduce heat and cook, covered, for about 20 minutes.

3. Return fish to the pan, baste with the sauce, cover and cook until the fish are well heated, about 3 minutes. Sprinkle with fresh parsley and serve.

RED MULLET WITH OLIVES

triglie alla ligure

INGREDIENTS:

12 large, fresh red mullet
1/2 cup fine olive oil
1 1/2 cups dry white wine
5 oz. pitted black olives
3 chopped garlic cloves
1 lemon, cut into halves
Salt and freshly ground black
  pepper
2 chopped tablespoons parsley

1. Preheat oven to medium-high (400° F., 200° C.). Arrange fish in one layer in a large ovenproof dish.

2. Pour over the olive oil and wine. Sprinkle the olives and garlic over the fish and place the lemon halves on top, cut side down. Season with salt and pepper. Cover with foil and bake for 10-15 minutes, depending on size.

3. Remove the fish from the baking pan and keep hot. Transfer the baking juices to a small saucepan and cook until reduced to half. Pour the sauce over fish, sprinkle with chopped parsley and serve.

HOT RED MULLET IN OLIVE OIL AND HERBS

triglie sapre

INGREDIENTS:

12 fresh red mullet
1/2 cup olive oil
3 chopped garlic cloves
1 fresh hot chili pepper, chopped
Salt and freshly ground black
  pepper
4 tablespoons mixed fresh herbs
  (parsley, basil, sage, thyme etc.)
Juice of 1 lemon

1. Heat olive oil in a wide frying pan. Fry garlic and hot pepper for 2-3 minutes.

2. Add fish and fry for about 2 minutes on each side. Season with salt and pepper.

3. Add mixed herbs and lemon juice, cover and cook for 1-2 minutes. Serve at once.

RED MULLET IN GRAPEVINE LEAVES

INGREDIENTS:

12 small fresh red mullet
½ cup quality olive oil
Juice of 1 lemon
2 tablespoons chopped parsley
1 tablespoon chopped dill
1 tablespoon chopped basil
Salt and freshly ground black
  pepper
12 large grapevine leaves, fresh or
  preserved in brine

1. Mix olive oil, lemon juice and herbs in a bowl, and season with salt and pepper. Add fish and leave to marinate for an hour or two.

2. Blanch grapevine leaves in boiling water for 1 minute. Remove, rinse, and drain.

3. Put a fish at the base of each leaf, roll up, and wrap fish completely. Brush each leaf with olive oil.

4. Charcoal-grill the wrapped fish for 2-3 minutes on each side, or place under a broiler for about 2 minutes on each side. Serve at once.

The grapevine leaves add flavor, as well as protecting the fish from directly touching the hot coals.

FISH BAKED IN FOIL

pesce al forno

INGREDIENTS:

6 fresh whole fish (bass, grey
    mullet, trout)
2 carrots, diced
1 onion, finely chopped
2 celery stalks, thinly sliced
6 tablespoons olive oil
Juice of 1 lemon
Salt and freshly ground black
    pepper
2 chopped garlic cloves
3 tablespoons mixed herbs
    (parsley, basil, thyme etc.)

1. Preheat oven to medium-high
(400° F., 200° C.). On a work
surface, lay out 6 sheets of foil,
each large enough to entirely
enclose a fish. Spread a mixture of
the carrots, onion and celery along
the center of each sheet. Place a
fish on top of the vegetables. Lift
edges of foil around the fish, to
make a boat-like shape.

2. Sprinkle each fish with olive oil,
a little lemon juice, salt, pepper, a
little garlic, and ½ tablespoon of
the mixed herbs.

3. Fold edges of foil over the fish
and secure tightly.

4. Bake for 15-20 minutes,
according to type and size of fish.

BAKED FISH WITH TOMATOES

pesce al forno con pomodore

INGREDIENTS:

6 whole fish (grey mullet, bass)
½ cup olive oil
8 firm, ripe tomatoes, sliced
2 onions, thinly sliced
4 crushed garlic cloves
3 tablespoons chopped parsley
Salt and freshly ground black
    pepper
½ cup dry white wine
Juice of 1 lemon

1. Preheat oven to medium-high
(400° F., 200° C.). Oil a heat-proof
baking pan, large enough to hold
the fish in one layer. Arrange half
the tomatoes, onion, garlic and
parsley at bottom of pan and
season with salt and pepper.

2. Arrange fish in the pan, season
with salt and pepper and rub with
garlic. Cover with remaining tomato
and onion slices, garlic, and
parsley. Season again with salt and
pepper.

3. Mix oil, wine and lemon juice in
a bowl and pour over the fish.

4. Bake for 30-40 minutes,
depending on the size of fish.

SOLE FLORENTINE

INGREDIENTS:

6 fillets of sole
2 lbs. fresh spinach leaves, washed
    and cleaned
2 oz. butter
1 chopped garlic clove
Salt and freshly ground black
    pepper
Ground nutmeg
½ cup dry white wine
1 cup cream
3 tablespoons grated Parmesan

1. Cook spinach in boiling salted
water for 3 minutes. Drain and
squeeze out as much moisture as
possible. Chop coarsely.

2. Melt half the butter in a frying
pan, add garlic and onion, and
sauté for about 2 minutes. Season
with salt, pepper, and nutmeg. Add
wine and cook for 1 minute, then
add cream, and cook another
2 minutes. Add spinach and stir.

3. Preheat oven to medium-high
(400° F., 200° C.). Spread the
spinach at the bottom of a
heat-proof dish large enough to
hold the fish in one layer. Arrange
fish on top of spinach and press
slightly into the spinach. Season
with salt and pepper, dot with
remaining butter, sprinkle with
Parmesan and bake for about
15 minutes.

SEA BASS WITH POTATOES

INGREDIENTS:

6 fillets of sea bass, unskinned
2 lbs. potatoes
½ cup olive oil
Salt and freshly ground black
*   pepper*
2 chopped garlic cloves
⅓ cup dry white wine

1. Peel potatoes and slice thinly. Soak in cold water for 1 hour, drain and pat dry.

2. Preheat oven to medium-high (400° F., 200° C.). Arrange potato slices at the bottom of a large baking dish. Pour all but
1 tablespoon of the olive oil over the potatoes, season with salt and pepper and sprinkle with garlic. Bake in preheated oven for about 20 minutes.

3. Brush fish with remaining olive oil, then season with salt and pepper. Place fish on top of potato layer, pour over wine and bake a further 10-15 minutes.

SALMON IN BUTTER AND SAGE

salmone al burro e salvia

INGREDIENTS:

6 salmon steaks, 1/2 inch thick
Salt and freshly ground black
pepper
2 oz. butter
12 fresh sage leaves

1. Season the steaks with salt and pepper.

2. Melt butter in a frying pan large enough to hold all six steaks. Add 6 of the sage leaves, and place, well spaced in pan. Chop remaining sage. When butter is very hot, place a steak on each leaf, sprinkle remaining sage on top and fry for 3 minutes on each side.

3. Transfer fish and fried sage leaves to a serving dish, and serve hot.

FISH STEAKS WITH CAPERS

INGREDIENTS:

6 sea bass steaks
1/2 cup dry white wine
Juice of 1 lemon
1 tablespoon chopped rosemary
    leaves
4 chopped garlic cloves
1 tablespoon chopped parsley
Salt and freshly ground black
    pepper
1/3 cup olive oil
2 tablespoons breadcrumbs
3 tablespoons chopped capers

1. Mix wine, lemon juice, rosemary, garlic and parsley in a bowl, season with salt and pepper, and allow fish to marinate in the mixture for 2 hours.

2. Heat oil in a frying pan and fry fish steaks on both sides. Sprinkle with breadcrumbs and capers, turn and sprinkle other side with breadcrumbs and capers. Pour over a little of the marinade every few moments, to keep the fish moist.

3. When fish are almost done, add remaining marinade, cook for 1-2 minutes and serve.

SARDINES IN HOT SAUCE

INGREDIENTS:

30 fresh sardines
A little plain white flour
Salt and freshly ground black
    pepper
1/3 cup olive oil

SAUCE:

1/3 cup olive oil
1 large onion, finely chopped
1/2 a cup wine vinegar
Salt and freshly ground black
    pepper
4-6 chopped garlic cloves
1 fresh hot chili pepper, chopped
1/4 cup chopped mint leaves

1. Season flour with salt and pepper. Flour sardines and shake to remove excess flour. Heat olive oil in a frying pan. When sizzling, add sardines and fry for 1-2 minutes on each side.

2. Prepare the sauce: Heat olive oil in a separate pan, add chopped onion and sauté for about 10 minutes. Add vinegar, season with salt and pepper, and cook until most of the vinegar has evaporated.

3. Add garlic, pepper and mint, stir and cook a further 1-2 minutes.

4. Transfer sardines to a shallow serving dish, pour sauce on top, and set aside for 2 hours. Add a little olive oil before serving.

STUFFED SARDINES

INGREDIENTS:

30 fresh whole sardines

STUFFING:

2-3 slices bread, soaked in water
    and squeezed
1/2 cup chopped parsley
2 chopped garlic cloves
1/2 cup grated Parmesan
1 egg
Salt and freshly ground black
    pepper
A little flour
Salt and freshly ground black
    pepper
Olive oil
3 lemons, quartered

1. Clean and rinse sardines. Using a small pair of scissors, cut backbone next to the head and remove.

2. Place all ingredients for the stuffing in a bowl, mix until smooth, and stuff the fish.

3. Season flour with salt and pepper, and lightly flour stuffed fish.

4. Heat 1 inch of olive oil in a frying pan. When hot, fry the fish for 2 minutes on each side. Serve with quartered lemons.

Very delicate, surprisingly rich
– the tuna-fish mousse is
"walled" within the thin green
beans, and the result is well
worth the effort.

TUNA MOUSSE WITH GREEN BEANS

INGREDIENTS:

10 oz. can of tuna in olive oil
1 cup cream
5 oz. softened butter
Salt and freshly ground black
  pepper
1 teaspoon dried thyme
1 lb. green beans
1 medium beetroot, peeled
Serve with quality olive oil

1. Place tuna in a food-processor and work to a smooth puree. Slowly add cream and butter, season with salt and pepper, and add thyme. Chill.

2. Trim the beans. Cook in boiling salted water for 7-8 minutes, or until beans are quite tender; in a separate pan, cook beetroot in water for about 15 minutes, or until quite tender. Rinse, allow to cool and slice thinly.

3. Place a beetroot slice at the bottom of 6 individual soufflé dishes, about 3 inches in diameter. Carefully arrange beens around sides of dishes, to make a "wall" that reaches the rim.

4. Fill the lined dishes with tuna mousse, press and chill for about 3 hours.

5. To serve, pour a little olive oil on a serving plate, and invert mousse dishes over each plate to release mousse.

GRILLED GREY MULLET

INGREDIENTS:

6 grey mullet
1/2 cup olive oil
Juice of 1 lemon
4 tablespoons chopped dill
1/2 bay leaf
2 chopped garlic cloves
*Salt and freshly ground black
   pepper*

1. Mix the oil, lemon, dill, bay leaf, garlic, salt, and pepper in a bowl, pour over fish, and allow to marinate for an hour.

2. Grill fish over charcoal fire or under an electric grill for 7-8 minutes on each side. Brush with marinade every once in a while during cooking.

SOLE WITH ZUCCHINI

INGREDIENTS:

12 fillets of sole
*6 tiny zucchini, sliced thinly
   lengthwise*
1 1/2 oz. butter
2 scallions (roots only)
4 tablespoons dry white vermouth
*Salt and freshly ground black
   pepper*

1. Preheat oven to very high (525 °F., 250° C.). Butter an ovenproof dish, large enough to hold fish in one layer, and arrange the zucchini, sliced very thinly lengthwise. Sprinkle chopped shallots over the zucchini, place fish on top and season with salt and pepper. Pour vermouth and dot with butter.

2. Bake for 5-6 minutes. Transfer to serving plates and serve at once. A little olive oil may be dribbled over fish before serving.

GREY MULLET IN GARLIC SAUCE

INGREDIENTS:

6 grey mullet, approximately 10 oz. each
1/3 cup olive oil
Juice of 1 lemon
Salt and freshly ground black pepper

SAUCE:

5-6 garlic cloves, peeled
3 tablespoons breadcrumbs
2 tablespoons chopped parsley
2 tablespoons vinegar
Salt and freshly ground black pepper
1/2 cup quality olive oil

1. Make 3-4 cuts along both sides of each fish.

2. Mix oil, lemon juice, salt and pepper and brush fish thoroughly with mixture.

3. Arrange fish in a single layer in a heat-proof dish and grill for 10-12 minutes on each side.

4. Meanwhile, prepare the sauce: Place garlic, breadcrumbs, parsley, and vinegar in a food-processor fitted with a steel blade. Season with salt and pepper and work to a smooth puree, gradually adding olive oil.

5. Serve the fish with a generous serving of sauce on top.

FRIED FISH STICKS

INGREDIENTS:

2 lbs. assorted fish fillets (red and grey mullet, sea bass)
Juice of 1 lemon
3 tablespoons dry white wine
Salt and freshly ground black pepper
1/2 cup flour
1/2 cup breadcrumbs
2 tablespoons mixed dried herbs
2 tablespoons chopped parsley
3 lemons, quartered
Oil for deep frying

1. Use at least three kinds of fish. Remove all skin and bone, then cut into 1×2 1/2 inch sticks.

2. Place fillet pieces in a bowl, pour lemon juice and wine on top, season with salt and pepper and mix well. Marinate for an hour.

3. Mix flour, breadcrumbs and herbs in a large bowl. Season with salt and pepper.

4. Drain fish sticks and toss thoroughly in the flour until completely covered.

5. Heat oil for deep frying, and fry 8-10 fish sticks at a time until well browned. Remove with a slotted spoon and drain on paper towels. Repeat until all fish sticks are cooked.

6. Transfer to a large serving dish, sprinkle with parsley and garnish with quartered lemons.

GRILLED FISH ON SKEWERS

INGREDIENTS:

1 1/2 lbs. fish fillets (sea bass, cod or a mixture of both)
1/3 cup olive oil
Juice of 1 lemon
3 tablespoons dry white wine
2 tablespoons chopped parsley
1 tablespoon chopped sage
1 tablespoon chopped basil
Salt and freshly ground black pepper
5 oz. fresh, small, whole button mushrooms

1. Cut fish into 1 1/4 inch squares.

2. Mix olive oil, lemon juice, wine and herbs in a bowl. Season with salt and pepper. Add fish, mix well and marinate for about half an hour.

3. Alternately skewer fish and mushrooms on wooden skewers. Grill on charcoal or broil for 2-3 minutes on each side and serve.

SALMON MOUSSE IN CREAM AND CHIVES SAUCE

INGREDIENTS:

1¼ lbs. fresh salmon fillets
1 oz. butter
1 small onion, very finely chopped
Salt and freshly ground black
  pepper
2 tablespoons flour
½ cup dry white wine
1 egg, beaten
1 cup cream

SAUCE:

1 cup cream
Salt and freshly ground black
  pepper
1 tablespoon lemon juice
3 tablespoons finely chopped
  chives

1. Place raw fish in a food-processor and work to a very smooth puree. Transfer to a bowl.

2. Melt butter in a frying pan and sauté onion until soft. Season with salt and pepper. Add flour and stir until flour turns a light gold color. Add wine and cook for about 3 minutes.

3. Add contents of frying pan to fish puree and stir. Add the beaten egg and cream, and mix well. Chill.

4. Preheat oven to medium-low (300° F., 160° C.). Butter six individual heat-proof ramekins, and fill each with the mousse mixture.

5. Pour a little water into the bottom of a large larg pan and arrange ramekins in it. Bake for about 25 minutes.

6. Meanwhile, prepare the sauce: In a small saucepan, cook the cream for a few minutes until slightly thickened. Season with salt and pepper, add lemon juice and chives, and cook for another minute.

7. Divide the sauce among six small, flat plates. Turn the contents of a ramekin onto the sauce and serve.

The white wine was made of the grapes growing around Vernaccia, an inn near San Gimignano.

SOLE ROLLED WITH VEGETABLES

INGREDIENTS:

8 fillets of sole
2 carrots
2 celery stalks
2 small zucchini
3 oz. softened butter
Salt and freshly ground black
*   pepper*
1/2 cup dry white wine

1. Cut each fillet in half, lengthwise.

2. Peel the carrots and cut lengthwise into "sticks" about 1/4 inch thick and 1 1/4-2 inches long. Cook carrot sticks in boiling salted water for 3-4 minutes, remove and drain well. Slice celery and zucchini in the same manner.

3. Place all the vegetables with 1 oz. butter in a frying pan and sauté for about 5 minutes. Season with salt and pepper and allow to cool.

4. Place a carrot, a celery and a zucchini "stick" at the edge of each fish fillet, roll up fish around vegetables and secure with a wooden toothpick.

5. Preheat oven to medium (350° F., 180° C.). Butter an ovenproof casserole and arrange fish rolls in it. Dot each roll with remaining butter, season with salt and pepper and pour wine into dish.

6. Bake for 10-15 minutes, and serve at once.

MEAT

The variety of meat dishes in the Italian cuisine serves to demonstrate its origins in the kitchens of the aristocracy as well as and in those of the poorer social strata. On one hand rich, expensive cuts of meat, lightly spiced and roasted on a charcoal fire; and on the other, the leftovers – inferior cuts and offal, heavily spiced and requiring lengthy cooking. Both kinds have given the Italian cuisine some of its most famous dishes:

The renowned Bistecca alla Fiorentina, the best cut, in the ideal thickness (very thick!), marvelously prepared (over charcoal!) and cooked to perfection (rare!) glorious, meaty, tasty and juicy; the stews require lengthy cooking, designed to tenderize inferior cuts, and heavily spiced – a trick which originally served to disguise the taste of the meat; and tripe – cow's stomach, which the Italians have turned into a delicacy.

Meat, like any other dish, varies regionally: in the south, mutton and a little goat's meat is used in preference to beef, which is hardly ever eaten. Veal dominates the central regions, as well as the north, although in the latter one may encounter the redder meat of more mature beef.

The Italians, one may say, are not very carnivorous. They specialize in veal, which they endeavor to refine, rather than stress its meatiness. The escalopes are cut thinly, all roasting or cooking are light and subdued, and highly suited to the nature of veal.

In the south, where mutton is usually eaten, cooking is cruder. Either the whole animal is grilled on a huge spit, turning slowly, shiny and dripping with fat, or it is cut into portions and then grilled. The further one goes north, the mutton is replaced with younger lambs and the dishes grow more refined: delicately spiced lamb chops, tiny legs fragrant with herbs, excellent short roasting that is the secret to the whole business. Even the cruder dishes are magnificent.

Cooking on charcoal fire is usually prefered to a gas fire – a real wood fire, that endows the roasting meat with its typical aroma. All kinds of meat and poultry are subjected to this delicious treatment. It is quite the best way to handle meat.

Carpaccio is Italy's contribution to universal culinary repertiore – thin slices of raw, aged red meat. They are eaten as they are, lightly spiced, and accompanied, naturally, by olive oil and some herbs: the meat used is obviously the best cuts – fillet or sirloin, free of tendons and fat. Pure meat. Pure pleasure.

Poultry is used often, in all regions, served fried, roasted, or cooked. Dishes are mostly simple, excellently treated and spiced to enhance the flavor of the bird, and the results are surprising. Restaurants serve more sophisticated dishes influenced by the Nouvelle Cuisine. The Italian chefs apply the principles of the Nouvelle Cuisine on classic Italian dishes, usually very successfully.

LEMON CHICKEN

INGREDIENTS:

1 chicken, cut into six pieces
½ cup quality olive oil
Juice of 1 lemon
3 chopped garlic cloves
3 tablespoons chopped parsley
1 tablespoon finely chopped basil
Salt and freshly ground black
_   pepper_
1 lemon (unpeeled), thinly sliced

1. Clean chicken and wipe dry.

2. Mix the olive oil, lemon juice, garlic, parsley, basil, salt, and pepper in a large ovenproof baking pan. Add chicken, coat each piece well and set aside to marinate for a few hours.

3. Preheat oven to medium-high (400° F., 200° C.), and bake the chicken for about 30 minutes. Turn occasionally, basting with the pan juices.

4. Arrange lemon slices on top of the chicken, baste again with pan juices and bake a further 15-20 minutes.

CHERRY CHICKEN

pollo con ciliege

INGREDIENTS:

6 chicken breasts, with skins and
_   bone)_
1 cup dry red wine
1 cup chicken stock
8 oz. cherries, pitted
1 tablespoon dried thyme
Salt and freshly ground black
_   pepper_
1 + 2½ oz. softened margarine

1. Prepare the sauce: Place wine, stock, cherries and thyme in a saucepan. Add some salt and pepper and bring to a boil. Reduce heat and cook until reduced by half. Reserving a few whole cherries, puree remaining cherries in a food-processor. Return pureed cherries to saucepan and stir.

2. Stir 2 oz. of the margarine into sauce until melted, making sure sauce does not reach boiling point.

3. Season chicken breasts with salt and pepper. Melt remaining ounce of margarine in a frying pan and fry chicken breasts for 3-4 minutes on each side.

4. Transfer chicken breasts to a serving plate. Pour sauce over breasts, garnish with reserved cherries, and serve.

Sergio's in Florence. Sergio, the owner and chef, is also a local councilman. He adds a creative touch to traditional Tuscan dishes.

CHICKEN WITH LENTILS

pollo con lenticchie

INGREDIENTS:

1 fresh young chicken, cut into
6 pieces
8 oz. lentils (brown or green)
3 tablespoons olive oil
2 oz. smoked beef, cut into thin
strips
1 onion, finely chopped
2 chopped garlic cloves
2 celery stalks, thinly sliced
Salt and freshly ground black
pepper

1. Soak lentils in water for an hour. Drain and rinse.

2. Heat oil in a deep, heavy pot, add chicken and brown well on all sides. Remove the chicken with a slotted spoon.

3. Add the smoked beef, onion, garlic and celery to the pot and sauté for about 10 minutes.

4. Add lentils and mix well. Add chicken and enough water to cover lentils, season with salt and pepper, and bring to a boil. Reduce heat and cook for about 45 minutes, or until the lentils are tender. If necessary, add a little water during cooking.

CHICKEN IN TOMATOES

pollo con pomodore

INGREDIENTS:

1 fresh young chicken, in
   6 pieces
Salt and freshly ground black
   pepper
1/3 cup quality olive oil
2 chopped garlic cloves
1 red onion, diced
2 celery stalks, thinly sliced
1 carrot, diced
2 tablespoons mixed dried herbs
   (basil, thyme, rosemary etc.)
1/2 small chili pepper, chopped
   (optional)
6 tomatoes, blanched, peeled, and
   finely chopped
1 cup dry white wine
A little finely chopped parsley

1. Season chicken with salt and
pepper. Heat oil in a deep
casserole with cover, add chicken,
and fry on all sides until well
browned. Remove from pan.

2. Add garlic, onion, celery and
carrot to casserole and sauté for
about 10 minutes. Stir occasionally.

3. Return chicken to casserole, add
herbs and hot pepper.

4. Add tomatoes and wine and
bring to a boil. Reduce heat, cover
casserole and cook for
30-40 minutes. Sprinkle with
chopped parsley before serving.

FRIED CHICKEN WITH ZUCCHINI AND ARTICHOKE HEARTS

pollo con zucchini e carciofi

INGREDIENTS:

1 fresh young chicken, cleaned
3 artichokes
3 small, firm zucchini
1/2 lemon
2 eggs, beaten
2 tablespoons finely chopped
   parsley
Salt and freshly ground black
   pepper
3 lemons, quartered
Olive oil
1 cup flour

1. Using kitchen scissors, cut
chicken, with bones, into small
slices, 1 inch wide and 2 1/2 inches
long.

2. Remove and discard outer leaves
of artichokes, cut artichokes into
quarters, discard the fuzzy inner
choke, and rub with half a lemon to
prevent discoloring.

3. Slice zucchini diagonally into
1/2 an inch slices.

4. Beat the eggs and parsley
together in a wide bowl, and
season with salt and pepper.

5. Heat 1 1/4 inches of olive oil in a
deep frying pan, until sizzling.

6. Dip the chicken pieces in flour,
then in the egg mixture and again
in the flour. Fry on both sides until
brown and crisp.

7. Coat and fry artichoke quarters
and zucchini in the same manner.

8. Arrange on a large serving dish,
and serve accompanied by lemon
quarters.

CHICKEN HUNTER'S STYLE

pollo alla cacciatora

INGREDIENTS:

1 small, fresh chicken
Salt and freshly ground black
   pepper
2 sprigs rosemary, or 1 tablespoon
   dried
2 sprigs sage, or 1 tablespoon
   dried
2 sprigs thyme, or 1 tablespoon
   dried
1/4 cup olive oil
1 celery stalk, thinly sliced
1 carrot, chopped
1 onion, finely chopped
1 1/2 cups dry white wine

SAUCE:

6 shallots, finely chopped
1 oz. margarine
2 tablespoons vinegar
1 egg yolk
Salt and freshly ground black
   pepper

1. Season chicken with salt and
pepper, and stuff stomach cavity
with the herbs.

2. Heat oil in a deep casserole, and
brown the chicken well on all sides.

3. Add the celery, carrot, onion and
wine and bring to a boil. Reduce
heat, cover and cook for
30-40 minutes. Remove from fire,
take the chicken out of the sauce
and keep warm. Strain the liquids in
which chicken has been cooked.

4. Prepare the sauce: Sauté
chopped shallots in margarine for
about 10 minutes.

5. Put the strained liquids in which
chicken has been cooked into a
small saucepan, add the sautéed
shallots and vinegar, and cook until
reduced to half.

6. Put 2 tablespoons of the sauce into a small bowl and beat the egg yolk into it. Stir this yolk mixture back into sauce and season with salt and pepper.

7. Cut chicken into serving pieces, pour over sauce, and serve.

GRILLED DEVILLED CHICKEN

pollo alla diavolo

INGREDIENTS:

1 fresh young chicken, cut in
   6 servings, or 6 legs of chicken
2 tablespoons quality olive oil
Juice of 1 lemon
1/2 cup dry white wine
1/2 hot chili pepper, chopped
Salt and freshly ground black
   pepper
2-3 sprigs fresh rosemary, or
   1 teaspoon dried

1. Clean chicken and wipe dry.

2. Mix the other ingredients in an ovenproof dish. Add chicken, turn to coat well and allow to marinate for 2 hours. Baste the chicken every once in a while.

3. The chicken may be grilled in two ways:

Under an electric broiler: place the dish containing chicken under preheated grill, not too close, so as not to scorch it, and grill for about 40 minutes, turning occasionally. Baste chicken every once in a while with pan juices.

On a charcoal fire: remove chicken from pan, place on a charcoal grill, skin side down, and grill, turning over every once in a while, for about 1/2 hour, or until chicken is done. During cooking, brush often with marinade.

CHICKEN WITH PINE NUTS AND RAISINS

pollo alla montanura

INGREDIENTS:

6 legs of chicken, or 1 chicken cut
   into 6 servings
1/2 cup olive oil
1 cup dry red wine
2 tablespons vinegar
1 sprig thyme, or 1 teaspoon dried
1 sprig rosemary, or 1 teaspoon
   dried
1 bay leaf
1 tablespons grated orange peel
2 whole cloves
1 red onion, diced
1 chopped garlic clove
Salt and freshly ground black
   pepper
1 1/2 oz. raisins
1 1/2 oz. pine nuts

1. Mix the oil, wine, vinegar, thyme. rosemary, bay leaf, orange peel, cloves, onion, and garlic in an ovenproof dish. Season with salt and pepper. Add chicken, baste well and allow to marinate overnight.

2. Just before cooking, add raisins and pine nuts.

3. Preheat oven to medium-high (400° F., 200° C.). Place chicken, skin side up, and bake for about 45 minutes. Baste occasionally with pan juices.

STUFFED CHICKEN BREASTS WITH HERB FILLING

fetti di pollo ripieni

INGREDIENTS:

6 breasts of chicken
3/4 cup quality olive oil
1 large onion, chopped
2 chopped garlic cloves
3 oz. fresh button mushrooms,
   finely chopped
Salt and freshly ground black
   pepper
3 tablespoons chopped parsley
1 tablespoon chopped basil
1 tablespoon fresh thyme leaves, or
   1 teaspoon dried
1 handful fresh tarragon leaves, or
   1 teaspoon dried
2 eggs
1 cup breadcrumbs
3 lemons, quartered

1. Prepare the stuffing: heat 1/4 cup of the olive oil in a frying pan, add onion and garlic and saute for about 10 minutes. Add mushrooms, season with salt and pepper and sauté an additional 2 minutes. Add herbs, stir for 1 minute, remove from heat and allow to cool.

2. Using a small, sharp knife, carefully make a cut at the thick side of each breast, to make a "pocket".

3. Fill each pocket with the stuffing.

4. Beat eggs well in a bowl. Place breadcrumbs in a deep bowl.

5. Dip each stuffed chicken breast in the eggs, then in breadcrumbs, and fry in the remaining olive oil for about 3 minutes on each side.

6. Serve hot, garnished with quartered lemons.

STUFFED CHICKEN NECKS

Getting suitable necks requires a little effort: ask the butcher to cut the necks as close as possible to the body.

INGREDIENTS:

6 chicken necks, with skin
1½ lbs. slightly fat veal, minced twice
1 chopped garlic clove
1 tablespoon green peppercorns (optional)
3 tablespoon quality olive oil
2 tablespoons chopped parsley
Salt and freshly ground black pepper

1. Carefully "peel" the skin from necks, folding it backwards. Cut off and discard bones and meat, so that only a "sleeve" of skin remains.

2. Mix minced veal, garlic, peppercorns, oil and parsley in a bowl and season with salt and pepper.

3. Stuff each neck with the meat mixture and sew the ends securely.

4. Cook stuffed neck in stock or water for about 20 minutes, making sure liquids simmer gently just below boiling point.

5. To serve: allow to cool slightly, slice into ½ an inch pieces, arrange on a serving dish, and serve with olive oil mayonaise.

OLIVE OIL MAYONAISE

Using a hand held mixer, beat 2 egg yolks. Gradually add 1¼ cups quality olive oil, beating all the time, until mixture thickens. Add juice of ½ a lemon, ½ a teaspoon mustard and salt and pepper.

Cocks' necks stuffed with minced veal, accompanied by fresh olive oil mayonnaise.

BREAST OF DUCK IN SHALLOT SAUCE

petti d'anitra

INGREDIENTS:

*6 breasts of duck (muscovy duck),
    with fatty skin*
1 oz. margarine
5 shallots, finely chopped
2 tablespoons wine vinegar
1 cup dry red wine
1 cup chicken stock
*1 fresh sprig thyme, or 1 teaspoon
    dried*
*1 fresh sprig rosemary, or
    1 teaspoon dried*
*Salt and freshly ground black
    pepper*

1. Prepare the sauce: Heat margarine in a frying pan, add shallots and sauté until soft. Add vinegar and cook for 5 minutes, until most of the vinegar has evaporated. Add wine, stock, thyme and rosemary and season with salt and pepper. Cook until liquid is reduced by half.

2. Heat dry a heavy frying pan, fry the breasts, skin side down, in their own fat for about 2 minutes on each side. Remove breasts from pan and discard all fat from the pan.

3. Return breasts to frying pan and pour the reduced sauce on top. Bring to a boil, lower heat and cook for about 15 minutes.

4. Cut breasts diagonally into thin slices and arrange on a serving plate. Pour the sauce over the slices and serve at once.

DUCK STUFFED WITH PRUNES AND CHESTNUTS

petti d'anitra ripieni

INGREDIENTS:

1 large duck or muscovy duck,
    about 4½ lbs.
1 cup dry red wine
7 oz. prunes
2 tablespoons olive oil
1 onion, chopped
1 lemon, halved and sliced
7 oz. shelled chestnuts
1 tablespoon fresh thyme, or
    1 teaspoon dried
Salt and freshly ground black
    pepper

1. Heat wine, remove from heat, add prunes and soak for an hour. Drain and reserve wine.

2. Heat olive oil in a frying pan and sauté onion until transparent.

3. Put the sautéed onion in a bowl with the drained prunes, the lemon slices, chestnuts and thyme and mix well.

4. Stuff duck with chestnut mixture.

5. Preheat oven to medium (350° F., 180° C.). Place stuffed duck in a roasting pan and season with salt and pepper. Roast for 30 minutes, then pour over the reserved wine. Bake for an additional 1-1½ hours. Baste duck often with pan juices.

6. Cut into servings and serve.

A food festival in Venice. Miles of tables along the piers, thousands of happy diners.

BRAISED VEAL SHANKS

ossobuco

The ossobucco, like the pizza, has turned into a symbol of Italian cooking.

INGREDIENTS:

6 veal shanks, about 2 inches thick
½ cup flour
Salt and freshly ground black
 pepper
½ cup quality olive oil
3 chopped garlic cloves
1 onion, chopped
6 tomatoes, coarsely chopped
2 tablespoons chopped parsley
1 cup dry white wine
1 tablespoon grated orange rind

1. Place flour on a plate and season with salt and pepper. Dip each piece of veal in flour and shake to remove excess.

2. Heat olive oil in a heavy iron pot with a cover. Add veal and fry, turning, until browned on all sides. Remove from pot.

3. Toss in garlic and onion and sauté for about 10 minutes.

4. Return the veal to pot, add half the tomatoes, all of the parsley, and all of the wine. Season with salt and pepper. Bring to a boil, reduce heat to a minumum and cook, covered, for about 1¼ hours.

5. Add remaining tomatoes and cook for 15 minutes.

6. Sprinkle remaining parsley and grated orange rind on top, cover, and cook for 5 minutes. Serve at once with peasant bread.

SLICED VEAL IN TUNA SAUCE

vitello tonnato

INGREDIENTS:

1¼ lbs. lean veal (rump, sirloin), in one piece
⅓ cup olive oil
Juice of 1 lemon
1 egg yolk
2 anchovy fillets
1 tablespoon capers
7 oz. light tuna in olive oil
Salt and freshly ground black pepper

1. Cook veal in stock or water, in a large saucepan, for no more than 10 minutes. Remove and allow to cool.

2. Place remaining ingredients in a food-processor fitted with a steel blade, and work to a smooth puree.

3. Slice the meat as thinly as possible. Arrange slices attractively on serving plates, and pour some of the sauce in the center. Garnish with a few capers and lemon wedges, and serve cold.

VEAL MEATBALLS IN FRESH TOMATO SAUCE

INGREDIENTS:

1¼ lbs. chopped veal
3 tablespoons olive oil
1 onion, finely chopped
2 tablespoons chopped parsley
1 tablespoon chopped basil
½ cup breadcrumbs
2 eggs
Salt and freshly ground black
   pepper
Oil for frying
Fresh tomato sauce (p. 92)

1. Fry the onion in the olive oil until golden.

2. Put the fried onion in a bowl and add the chopped veal, garlic, parsley, breadcrumbs, and eggs. Season with salt and pepper and mix until all ingredients are well blended.

3. Shape into balls about 1½ inches in diameter.

4. Heat 1 inch of olive oil in a deep frying pan. When sizzling, fry the meat balls, a few at a time, for 5-6 minutes until golden. Turn balls occasionally so they are well fried on all sides. Remove and drain on kitchen towels.

5. Pour fresh tomato sauce into a deep dish, arrange the meat balls on top and serve.

STUFFED BREAST OF VEAL

INGREDIENTS:

1 breast of veal, about 2-2½ lbs.
3 tablespoons olive oil
1 onion, finely chopped
2 chopped garlic cloves
3 chicken livers
½ lb. finely chopped veal
3 oz. fresh or frozen peas
1½ oz. pistachio nuts (unroasted),
   shelled and coarsely chopped
½ cup breadcrumbs
4 tablespoons finely chopped
   parsley
1 tablespoon fresh marjoram, or
   1 teaspoon dried
Salt and freshly ground black
   pepper
1 egg
2 tablespoons Marsala or port

1. Using a sharp knife, cut a slit at the side of the breast, to make "pocket" (or ask your butcher).

2. Heat olive oil in a frying pan, add chopped onion and garlic and sauté. Add livers and fry for 2-3 minutes. Remove, allow to cool and chop livers, reserving pan juices.

3. Place chopped veal, peas, nuts, breadcrumbs, parsley and marjoram in a bowl and season with salt and pepper. Add chopped liver, together with frying oil and onion. Add egg and Marsala or port and mix well.

4. Fill the veal pocket with this stuffing and sew the opening with needle and strong thread. Roll up breast and tie securely.

5. Fill a large saucepan with stock, or with water to which a carrot, an onion and a celery stalk have been added, and bring to a boil. Add veal, reduce heat slightly, and simmer, covered, for 1½ hours. Drain and refrigerate overnight. Cut into ½ an inch slices and serve.

VEAL BAKED WITH GRAPEVINE LEAVES AND MUSHROOMS

INGREDIENTS:

1 veal roast, about 3½ lbs., in one
    piece
12 grapevine leaves
7 oz. fresh, whole button
    mushrooms
6-8 dried porcini mushrooms,
    soaked in warm water and
    squeezed dry
⅓ cup olive oil
Juice of 1 lemon
2 tablespoons chopped parsley
3 chopped garlic cloves
Salt and freshly ground black
    pepper
2 sprigs fresh rosemary, or
    1 tablespoon dried
1 cup dry white wine

1. Preheat oven to medium-high (400° F., 200° C.). Rub a little olive oil over an oval ovenproof dish and line with with vine leaves. Spread the fresh and dried mushrooms around edges.

2. Place oil, lemon juice, parsley and garlic in a bowl, season with salt and pepper and beat slightly. Brush meat with this mixture, and place it in the baking dish. Top with rosemary sprigs and pour wine into bottom of dish.

3. Bake for 1-1½ hours, until roast is well browned, basting occasionally with pan juices. The roast can be served hot or cold.

_Rosemary sprigs, grapevine
leaves and porcini mushrooms
all add to the taste of this
juicy roast, just out of the
oven._

The Italians love grilling meats over burning logs: cocks, wild game, gigantic cuts of veal and beef. Cubes of bread, skewered between the meat, get toasted and flavored with the juices.

VEAL CHOPS WITH HERBS

costolette di vitello

INGREDIENTS:

6 veal chops, $3/4$ inch thick
$3/4$ cup breadcrumbs
Salt and freshly ground black
    pepper
2 tablespoons parsley, finely
    chopped
1 tablespoon fresh thyme, or
    1 teaspoon dried
1 tablespoon chopped basil
1 tablespoon chopped fresh sage,
    or 1 teaspoon dried
2 eggs
Olive oil for frying
2 lemons, quartered

1. Place breadcrumbs in a bowl, season with salt and pepper and add the chopped herbs.

2. Beat eggs in a second deep bowl.

3. Dip chops in beaten eggs, then in breadcrumbs. Make sure chops are evenly coated on all sides.

4. Heat oil for frying in a deep frying pan and fry chops for 3-4 minutes on each side, until coating is brown and crisp. Serve with quartered lemons.

BEEF AND BREAD SKEWERS

INGREDIENTS:

$1\frac{1}{2}$ lbs. sirloin
$1/2$ cup quality olive oil
Juice of $1/2$ lemon
3 chopped garlic cloves
2 tablespoons chopped parsley
1 tablespoon chopped fresh basil
Salt and freshly ground black
    pepper
18 slices of French bread, each
    1 inch thick
12 cherry tomatoes
12 baby onions

1. Cut meat into $1\frac{1}{2}$ inch cubes, leaving it fat-trimmed.

2. Place olive oil, lemon juice, garlic, parsley and basil in a bowl. Season with salt and pepper. Add cubed meat and allow to marinate for a few hours.

3. Alternately arrange a meat cube, a bread slice, an onion and a tomato on a skewer.

4. Grill over a charcoal fire or under an electric broiler for 7-8 minutes, turning occasionally. Brush with marinade every once in a while.

ESCALOPES OF VEAL WITH MUSHROOM STUFFING

INGREDIENTS:

6 very thin escalopes of veal
3½ oz. margarine
1 chopped garlic clove
1½ oz. smoked beef, cut into thin
_   strips_
5 oz. firm, fresh mushrooms,
_   coarsely chopped_
1 tablespoon fresh thyme leaves, or
_   1 teaspoon dried_
Salt and freshly ground black
_   pepper_
¾ cup dry red wine
1 whole sprig thyme (if available),
_   or another teaspoon dried thyme_

1. Prepare the stuffing: Heat 1 oz. margarine in a frying pan, add garlic and smoked beef and fry for about 3 minutes. Add mushrooms and thyme, season with salt and pepper and fry for 2 more minutes. Allow to cool.

2. Place some of the stuffing on each escalope, fold in half and secure with a toothpick.

3. Melt 1 oz. of margarine in frying pan and fry stuffed escalopes for 2-3 minutes on each side. Remove and keep hot.

4. Add wine and the sprig of thyme to frying pan and bring to a boil. Season with salt and pepper. Reduce pan juices to ¼ cup. Discard the thyme sprig.

5. Lower the heat and stir in 1½ oz. margarine, until melted. The sauce should not reach boiling point.

6. Transfer escalopes to a serving plate and pour sauce over.

ESCALOPES OF VEAL IN MARSALA

piccate al marsala

INGREDIENTS:

6 thin escalopes of veal
1/2 cup flour
Salt and freshly ground black
  pepper
1 1/2 oz. margarine
1/2 cup Marsala or Port

1. Place flour on a plate and season with salt and pepper.

2. Dip escalopes in flour and shake well to remove excess flour.

3. Melt margarine in a large, heavy frying pan. Add escalopes and fry for about 2 minutes on each side. Remove from pan and keep hot.

4. Add wine to frying pan and bring to a boil. Season with salt and pepper. Using a wooden spoon, scrape all the bits and pieces from the bottom of the pan and cook for about 5 minutes, until sauce is thick and syrupy.

5. Return escalopes to pan, cook for another minute and serve at once.

SALTIMBOCCA

INGREDIENTS:

6 thin escalopes of veal
6 thin slices smoked breast of
  goose
6 whole sage leaves
1 1/2 oz. margarine
1/2 cup Marsala or Port
Salt and freshly ground black
  pepper

1. Lay out escalopes, and place a slice of smoked breast and sage leaf on each. Roll the veal tightly and secure with a toothpick.

2. Melt margarine in a large, heavy frying pan. When very hot, fry veal rolls for about 2 minutes on all sides. Remove and keep hot.

3. Pour Marsala or port into frying pan and bring to a boil. Season with salt and pepper. Using a wooden spoon, scrape bits and pieces from the bottom of the pan and cook for about 5 minutes, until sauce is thick and syrupy.

4. Return veal rolls to the pan, cook for another minute and serve at once.

ESCALOPES OF VEAL IN LEMON SAUCE

scaloppine al limone

INGREDIENTS:

6 thin escalopes of veal, about
  5 oz. each
1/2 cup flour
Salt and freshly ground black
  pepper
2 1/2 oz. margarine
Juice of 1 lemon
1 tablespoon chopped parsley

1. Season flour with salt and pepper, dip escalopes and shake well to remove excess flour.

2. Melt 1 ounce of the margarine in a heavy frying pan, and when very hot fry escalopes for about about 2 minutes on each side. Remove from pan and keep warm.

3. Discard margarine and wipe pan dry. Melt remaining margarine, add the lemon juice, season with salt and pepper, and cook for about a minute.

4. Arrange escalopes on a serving dish, pour over lemon sauce, and sprinkle chopped parsley on top.

ESCALOPES OF VEAL IN HERBS

INGREDIENTS:

*6 thin escalopes of veal, about
    5 oz. each*
½ cup flour
*Salt and freshly ground black
    pepper*
⅓ cup quality olive oil
1 chopped garlic clove
*2 tablespoons mixed fresh herbs
    (basil, thyme, sage, parsley etc.)*
Juice of ½ lemon

1. Place flour on a plate and season with salt and pepper.

2. Dip escalopes in flour and shake to remove excess.

3. Heat olive oil in a frying pan. Add escalopes and fry for about 2 minutes on each side. Remove from pan and keep warm.

4. Add garlic and herbs to frying pan and stir for 1 minute. Add lemon juice, season with salt and pepper and pour over escalopes. Serve at once.

*Fox hunting on Saturday (left);
the cushion attests to the long
hours spent at the window.*

CARPACCIO

INGREDIENTS:

*1¼ lbs. fillet of beef, aged,
    trimmed of fat and tendons*
½ cup olive oil
*1 tablespoon crushed black
    peppercorns*
*2 tablespoons mixed fresh herbs
    (parsley, thyme, basil, sage etc.)*
20 basil leaves, cut into strips
2 tablespoons olive oil
A little lemon juice (optional)

1. Mix together the olive oil, pepper and herbs.

2. Place the meat in a plastic bag, add oil, close bag and shake well so that the meat is enclosed in oil. Refrigerate for a day or two.

3. Remove meat from bag, wipe pff remaining oil and place in the freezer until half frozen, in order to facilitate cutting into paper-thin slices.

4. Slice as thinly as possible. Arrange slices on serving plates, sprinkle with a little basil, parsley and lemon juice and serve at once.

Carpaccio relies mostly on the quality of the meat – prime beef, well aged. The dressing is simple – a little olive oil, a drop of lemon.

Ettore Silvestry, chairman of the Tuscan Vintners' Union, loves and knows wine. His restaurant, Anticca Trattoria Botteganove, boasts a rare collection of the finest wines of the region.

BEEF BRAISED IN RED WINE

INGREDIENTS:

2 lbs. beef (rump or topside)
2 celery stalks, thinly sliced
2 carrots, sliced
1 onion, chopped
3 chopped garlic cloves
1 bay leaf
1 sprig fresh rosemary, or
    1 teaspoon dried
2 whole cloves
3 cups dry red wine
Salt and freshly ground black
    pepper
Grated nutmeg
4 tablespoons olive oil
A little flour

1. Place all the ingredients, except 4 tablespoons of olive oil and the flour, in a bowl. Stir, add meat and refrigerate for 2 days. Turn occasionally.

2. Remove meat from marinade and wipe dry. Reserve marinade.

3. Dip meat in flour so it is coated on all sides. Heat oil in a large, heavy saucepan. When sizzling, add meat and fry on all sides.

4. Meanwhile, transfer marinade to a saucepan, bring to a boil and cook until reduced by half. Carefully add to the frying meat. Bring to a boil, reduce heat to a minimum and cook, covered, for 1½-2 hours, until tender.

5. Remove the meat and place the sauce with vegetables in a food-processor fitted with a steel blade. Work to a smooth puree, return to pot and heat.

6. Slice the meat into ½ inch slices, pour over the sauce and serve.

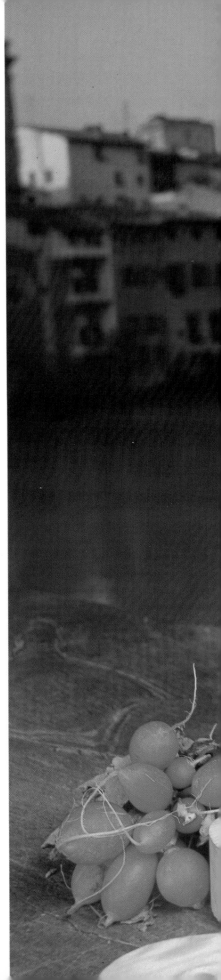

Above: Morning in the Florentine meat market. Below: Bistecca alla Fiorentina, and in the background, the Ponte Vecchio.

GRILLED STEAK

bistecca alla fiorentina

Ask your butcher for 2-3 T-bone cuts. Each steak should be 1¼-2 inches thick and weigh about 2 lbs. It should, of course, be properly aged, and on no account must the fat be removed. Brush the steaks with a little olive oil and season with pepper. Place over a charcoal fire and grill for 5-6 minutes on one side (do not move steaks while grilling). Turn on other side and grill for 5-6 more minutes. Remove from fire, season with a little salt and serve with ½ lemon on the side. The secret to a good Bistecca alla Fiorentina is choosing the proper cut and using the best available meat.

BRAISED BEEF GENOESE STYLE

INGREDIENTS:

A 3 lbs. chunk of veal or beef
    (rump or topside) secured with
    string
3 tablespoons olive oil
1 onion, finely chopped
1 chopped garlic clove
4 ripe tomatoes, peeled and
    chopped
2 celery stalks, thinly sliced
1 carrot, diced
1 cup dry white wine
1 tablespoon finely chopped basil
    leaves
Salt and freshly ground black
    pepper

1. Heat oil in a heavy casserole,
add garlic and onion and saute for
about 10 minutes.

2. Add meat and brown well on all
sides.

3. Add tomatoes, celery and carrot.
Add wine and basil, season with
salt and pepper, and bring to a boil.
Reduce heat to minimum and cook,
covered, for about 1½ hours.

TRIPE STEW

trippa

INGREDIENTS:

1½ lbs. tripe
3 tablespoons vinegar
4 tablespoons olive oil
1 chopped garlic clove
1 onion, chopped
1 carrot, diced
2 celery stalks, thinly sliced
1 lb. tomatoes, peeled and coarsely
    chopped
Salt and freshly ground black
    pepper
1 cup dry white wine
Chopped parsley

1. Rinse tripe thoroughly under
running water. Place in a bowl, add
vinegar and water to cover and
soak overnight. The next day rinse
again in plenty of water. Cut into
3-4 pieces and and cook in boiling
salted water for about an hour.
Remove from pan, rinse and drain.
Cut into long, thin strips.

2. Heat oil in a large saucepan, add
garlic, onion, carrot and celery and
sauté for about 10 minutes. Add
tomatoes, season with salt and
pepper and stir.

3. Add tripe, wine and 1 cup of
water and bring to a boil. Reduce
heat, cover and cook for about an
hour.

4. Transfer to a serving dish and
sprinkle with chopped parsley
before serving.

VEAL LIVER VENETIAN STYLE

INGREDIENTS:

1½ lbs. veal liver
1½ oz. margarine
2 large onions, thinly sliced
Salt and freshly ground black
    pepper
½ cup dry white wine
1 tablespoon finely chopped
    parsley

1. Cut liver into thin slices, then cut
each slice into strips ½ inch wide.

2. Melt half the margarine in a
frying pan, add onion and sauté
until lightly coloured. Season with
salt and pepper, add the wine and
bring to a boil. Reduce heat to
minimum and cook, covered, for
about 10 minutes. Remove from
frying pan and reserve.

3. Dry out the frying pan and heat
remaining margarine. When very
hot, add liver and fry until lightly
browned, stirring all the time. Add
onion and wine mixture, stir and
cook for another 2-3 minutes.

4. Before serving, sprinkle with a
little chopped parsley.

STEAK WITH TOMATOES AND GARLIC

bistecca alla pizzaiola

INGREDIENTS:

6 thick steaks (fillet or sirloin)
⅓ cup quality olive oil
2 3 crushed garlic cloves
10 ripe tomatoes, peeled and finely
   chopped
1 tablespoons chopped, fresh basil
   or oregano
Salt and freshly ground black
   pepper

1. Heat oil in a large, heavy frying pan with a cover, add steaks and fry for about a minute on each side. Remove and keep hot.

2. Add garlic to pan and fry lightly. Add tomatoes, basil or oregano, season with salt and pepper, cover and cook for 6-7 minutes.

3. Return the steaks to the pan and cover with sauce. Cover pan again and cook for 3-4 minutes.

FILLET OF BEEF BAKED IN SALT

INGREDIENTS:

6 thick fillet steaks, aged
5 tablespoons olive oil
4 shallots, coarsely chopped
18 fresh, firm mushrooms, thinly
    sliced
Salt and freshly ground black
    pepper
4 lbs. coarse salt
12 thin slices smoked beef
1 egg

1. Brush steaks with 2 tablespoons of the olive oil and season lightly with salt and pepper.

2. Heat remaining 3 tablespoons of olive oil in a frying pan, add chopped shallots and sauté. Add mushrooms and fry for 2-3 minutes. Season with salt and pepper and allow to cool slightly.

3. Preheat oven to very high (500° F., 250° C.). Spread a layer of coarse salt, ½ inch thick, at the bottom of an ovenproof dish. Place steaks in dish, slightly apart from each other.

4. Pile on each steak a "mound" of mushrooms, and cover these with 2 slices of smoked beef. Tuck edges of slices underneath the meat so that each steak is completely wrapped up.

5. Cover steaks completely with coarse salt – the dish should look as though it contains 6 mounds of salt.

6. Beat egg with 2 tablespoons water and use mixture to brush salt "mounds".

7. Bake 10 minutes for rare, 15 for well done.

8. Break the salt crust, remove steaks, shake off all traces of salt and serve at once.

The salt crust enveloping the meat, and in the background the campaniles of San Gimignano.

GRILLED VEAL AND PIGEON

INGREDIENTS:

2 pigeons or cornish hens
1½ lbs. veal

MARINADE FOR PIGEONS:

2 sprigs fresh rosemary, or
*   1 tablespoon dried*
1 cup dry red wine
⅓ cup olive oil
1 onion, finely chopped
2 chopped garlic cloves
1 crumbled bay leaf
Salt and freshly ground black
*   pepper*

MARINADE FOR VEAL:

½ cup dry white wine
Juice of 1 lemon
¼ cup olive oil
1 chopped garlic clove
1 tablespoon chopped parsley
1 tablespoon fresh thyme leaves, or
*   1 teaspoon dried*
Salt and freshly ground black
*   pepper*

1. Mix ingredients for pigeon marinade in a bowl; mix ingredients for veal marinade in a separate bowl. Marinate pigeons and veal overnight in respective marinades.

2. Remove from marinade and grill slowly over charcoal. Turn occasionally and brush veal and pigeons with respective marinades. Grill for 30-40 minutes.

3. Slice veal, cut pigeons into servings and serve.

LEG OF LAMB WITH ROSEMARY AND GARLIC

INGREDIENTS:

1 leg of lamb, around 5 lbs., boned
½ cup olive oil
4-6 crushed garlic cloves
Salt and freshly ground black
  pepper
2-3 sprigs fresh rosemary, or
  1 tablespoon dried
2 cups dry white wine

1. Ask butcher to bone leg of lamb. Preheat oven to very high (500° F., 250° C.).

2. Mix oil and garlic in a bowl and season with salt and pepper. Place half the rosemary and half the oil inside the boned leg of lamb. Roll up and tie securely with string.

3. Place the meat in a roasting pan and brush with remaining oil. Place remaining rosemary sprig on top, or sprinkle rosemary over.

4. Roast for about 20 minutes. Add one cup of wine, reduce oven temperature to medium (350° F., 180° C.) and roast for about an hour. Add a little more wine every once in a while.

5. Remove from pan, slice and serve.

LEG OF LAMB IN MINT

INGREDIENTS:

1 leg of lamb, 4-5 lbs.
½ cup quality olive oil
Juice of 1 lemon
4 crushed garlic cloves
½ cup chopped fresh mint leaves
Salt and freshly ground black
  pepper
2 celery stalks, finely chopped
2 carrots, diced
1 onion, finely chopped
1 cup dry white wine

1. Preheat oven to very high (500° F., 250° C.). Mix oil, lemon juice, garlic and mint in a bowl. Season with salt and pepper.

2. Line the bottom of a roasting pan with the chopped vegetables and place the leg of lamb on top. Brush the lamb with oil mixture.

3. Bake for about 20 minutes.

4. Reduce oven temperature to medium-high (400° F., 200° C.) and roast for another 45 minutes. Pour a little white wine into bottom of pan every once in a while. If leg is large, or if desired well done, add more wine.

GRILLED MUTTON CHOPS

INGREDIENTS:

12 mutton or lamb chops
1/3 cup olive oil
Juice of 1 lemon
2 chopped garlic cloves
1 tablespoon chopped parsley
1 tablespoon fresh rosemary,
　or 1 teaspoon dried
1 tablespoon chopped basil
Salt and freshly ground black
　pepper

1. Mix all ingredients, except chops, in a wide bowl. Add chops and allow to marinate for about 2 hours.

2. Grill chops over charcoal fire for 1-2 minutes on each side, or under an electric broiler for about 2 minutes on each side.

SHOULDER OF LAMB AND FENNEL STEW

INGREDIENTS:

1 4-5 lbs. shoulder of lamb, cut into
　2 inch chunks
1 large bunch wild fennel leaves, or
　2 fennel bulbs
1/2 cup olive oil
1 chopped garlic clove
1 onion, finely chopped
6 ripe tomatoes, peeled and finely
　chopped
1/2 cup dry white wine
Salt and freshly ground black
　pepper

1. Coarsely chop fennel leaves; if using fennel bulbs, slice and chop.

2. Heat olive oil in a heavy pot. Add garlic and onion and sauté. Add meat and brown.

3. Add tomatoes, season with salt and pepper, cover and cook for about 10 minutes.

4. Stir in fennel. Add wine, reduce heat to minimum and cook, covered, for 3/4-1 hour.

MUTTON WITH GREEN OLIVES

INGREDIENTS:

2 lbs. shoulder or leg of mutton,
　cut into 2 inch chunks
1/2 cup olive oil
2 chopped garlic cloves
Salt and freshly ground black
　pepper
1 cup dry white wine
1 sprig fresh rosemary,
　or 1 teaspoon dried
8 oz. green olives

1. Heat olive oil in a large, heavy pot. Add garlic and fry until golden.

2. Add meat and fry for a few minutes, until browned. Season with salt and pepper.

3. Add wine and rosemary and bring to a boil. Reduce heat and cook, covered, for about 30 minutes.

4. Add olives, stir and cook an additional 20 minutes.

ce-cream is Italy's foremost contribution to confectionery. The Italians, quite simply, invented it. It all started with crushed ice flavoured with bits of fruit, and developed through the ages into the delicate, deliciously soft ice-cream we know today. Even the most out-of-the-way places in Italy boast an enviable variety of ice-creams based on cream and eggs, as well as sherbets made of fresh fruit. And they are never disappointing. Chocolate, too, came to Europe via Italy. The splendid chocolate industry established in Turin during the Eighteenth century spread to the rest of Europe, and even Suchard, the Swiss chocolate king, studied the secrets of chocolate making in Turin.

Sweets play an important role in the cafes and restaurants of Italy. The Italian cafes are "an establishment", and some of them are ancient, elegant and world-famous. The Cafe Rivoire in the Piazza della Signoria in Florence offers a sweet and wonderfully aromatic chocolate drink, served either hot or cold under a mound of thick cream, which is probably a foretaste of paradise; cafe Florian in Venice boasts marvelous pastries along with its view of the crowded Piazza San Marco; and Rome has her own ancient and famous cafe, "Cafe Paris".

But you can find simpler, equally good cafes all over Italy. There the Italians sip their strong, fragrant coffee and enjoy a small pastry: a cream-filled brioche, crumbly biscuits dunked in wine, a glazed fruit tartlet or a rich cake.

In many restaurants, a rich display of desserts is placed next to the antipasti. These usually include a variety of cakes, tarts and cookies, since the Italians are experts at baking and confectionery making. The display is arranged around an enormous glass bowl containing fruit soup, as well as a mouthwatering selection of fresh fruit.

The fruits include berries in season, delicious purple figs in summer, pomegranates, peaches, cherries and many others. They are eaten as they are, or dipped in a little lemon juice and sugar. A bowl of pomegranate seeds flavoured with a little lemon juice, sugar and liqueur is a real delight.

Fresh fruits find their way into tarts. The harmonious combination of crumbly pastry and delicate custard blends beautifully with almost any fruit: apricots, peaches, figs, cherries, strawberries etc.

The pastries vary regionally. Siena's special sweet is Panforte – a heavy, spicy cake densely inlayed with almonds and peanuts; Prato is the birthplace of the dry almond biscuits, a true delight when dunked in Vin Santo – a fortified dessert wine. Italy is, no doubt, a paradise for sweet lovers – ice-creams, chocolate, cakes and fruit; on the street, at home and in restaurants; before the meal, after the meal and between courses.

PEARS BAKED IN WINE

INGREDIENTS:

6 large, ripe pears
2½ cups dry red wine
¾ cup sugar
1 vanilla pod, sliced open
Outer rind of one whole lemon, if
   possible in one piece

1. Preheat oven to medium
(350° F., 180° C.). Place wine,
sugar, vanilla pod, and lemon rind
in a baking dish large enough to
hold the pears. Add pears.

2. Bake for 1-1¼ hours, turning the
pears and rolling them in the wine
mixture every 15 minutes.

3. Place a single pear in the center
of a dessert plate, and pour over it
3-4 tablespoons of the wine sauce.
Serve hot or at room temperature.

APRICOT DELIGHT

INGREDIENTS:

1¼ lbs. whole fresh apricots
½ cup castor sugar
The outer rind of one lemon, if
    possible cut in a single strip
1 tablespoon unflavored gelatine
    powder
¼ cup hot water
2 cups whipping cream
½ cup castor sugar
Juice of 1 lemon
Grated rind of 1 lemon
Apricots to garnish

1. Blanch apricots for a few minutes in boiling water, drain and peel. Cut in halves and remove pits.

2. Put the sugar with 1½ cups of water and the lemon peel in a saucepan and bring to a boil. Add apricots, reduce heat and cook for 10 minutes. Drain, remove the lemon peel and allow to cool slightly.

3. Dissolve gelatine in ¼ cup hot water.

4. Beat cream until stiff.

5. Put apricots, castor sugar, lemon juice and grated lemon rind in a food-processor fitted with a steel blade, and blend to a smooth puree. Transfer to a large bowl.

6. Stir in dissolved gelatine. Fold in whipped cream, gently but thoroughly.

7. Pour into a decorative mould, cover with wax paper and chill for at least 6 hours.

8. To serve: dip mould for one second in boiling water and turn onto a serving plate. Garnish with halved apricots and, if available, apricot leaves.

The heart of beautiful Tuscany, at the home of Signora Aronella, whose noble Italian family has owned the estate for generations.

192

TIRAMISU

Literally "Pick-me-up!"

INGREDIENTS:

FOR THE CUSTARD:

4 egg yolks
3/4 cup sugar
*1/2 cup liqueur, either kirsch, rum,
    brandy or Grand Marnier*
1/4 cup strong espresso coffee
*1 cup mascarpone, or cream
    cheese mixed with a little cream*
1 egg white
1 cup double cream
1 scant teaspoon vanilla
5 oz. ladyfinger biscuits

1. Prepare a custard base: Beat egg yolks and sugar in a small saucepan until pale and fluffy. Place in top of a double boiler and continue beating. Gradually beat in a 1/3 cup of the liqueur and keep beating until mixture thickens. Chill.

2. Blend the coffee completely into the mascarpone.

3. Beat the egg white until stiff and fold into the custard. Beat cream with vanilla until stiff.

4. Dip biscuits in remaining liqueur.

5. Arrange half the biscuits at the bottom of a shallow dish, spread with half the coffee flavored cream, half the custard and half the whipped cream. Cover with remaining biscuits and spread remaining creams in the same order. Cover and chill for several hours before serving.

ZABAIONE

INGREDIENTS:

6 egg yolks
1 cup castor sugar
*1 cup Marsala or other dessert
    wine*

1. Beat egg yolks and sugar until pale and fluffy.

2. Put the mixture into the top of a double boiler with simmering water and beat for about 5 minutes.

3. Add a little dessert wine and continue to beat. Gradually add remaining wine and continue beating until Zabaione is quite thick.

4. Pour into large stemmed glasses and serve immediately.

STUFFED PEACHES

INGREDIENTS:

6 large, firm, ripe peaches
*1 1/2 oz. blanched almonds, finely
    chopped*
1/3 cup sugar
Grated rind of 1 lemon
1 teaspoon cocoa powder
3 oz. crumbled macaroons
*2 tablespoons almond or orange
    liqueur*
1 egg yolk
A little icing sugar
1 1/2 oz. softened butter

1. Preheat oven to medium (350° F., 180° C.). Rinse peaches, cut in half lengthwise and remove stones. Using a spoon, hollow out some of the flesh and chop.

2. Add the chopped almonds, sugar, grated lemon rind, cocoa powder, macaroons, liqueur and egg yolk to the chopped peaches and mix well.

3. Fill peach halves with mixture, sprinkle over a little icing sugar and place a cube of butter atop each peach half.

4. Butter an ovenproof dish and arrange peaches in it. Bake for 20-30 minutes, or until lightly browned. Remove from oven, transfer to a serving dish, sprinkle with a little icing sugar and serve.

CARAMELIZED ORANGES

INGREDIENTS:

6 oranges
1 cup sugar
1 cup water
Juice of ½ lemon
½ vanilla pod, sliced open
  lengthwise

1. Using a small, sharp knife, peel the rind of 2 of the oranges without the pith and cut into long, thin strips. Cook rind in boiling water for about 3 minutes, drain and rinse.

2. Peel all oranges carefully, removing all traces of pith but keeping the oranges whole.

3. Put sugar, water, lemon juice and vanilla pod together into a saucepan large enough to hold all the oranges, bring to a boil and cook until caramelized into a light sugar syrup.

4. Add the whole oranges and cook for about 5 minutes. Roll occasionally in syrup while cooking. Carefully transfer to a serving dish. Discard vanilla pod.

5. Cook the orange peel in the syrup for about 5 minutes, remove and use to garnish oranges. Pour syrup over oranges and serve very cold.

CREMA DI MASCARPONE

INGREDIENTS:

4 egg yolks
³/₄ cup castor sugar
2-3 tablespoons liqueur, either
  kirsch, rum, brandy or Grand
  Marnier
1 lb. mascarpone (or, if unavailable,
  soft cream cheese)

1. Beat yolks and sugar until pale and fluffy. Add liqueur and beat for 1-2 minutes.

2. Add mascarpone and fold carefully until evenly mixed.

3. Divide among several small glass bowls and chill for several hours before serving.

MERINGUES WITH LEMON CREAM

INGREDIENTS:

36 small meringues

LEMON CREAM:

4 egg yolks
³/₄ cup castor sugar
Juice of 1 lemon
Grated rind of 1 lemon

VANILLA CREAM:

4 egg yolks
³/₄ cup castor sugar
1½ cups milk
1 cup cream
1 vanilla pod, sliced open
  lengthwise

1. Prepare lemon cream: beat egg yolks and sugar until light and fluffy. Add lemon juice and grated lemon rind and beat for a few more seconds. Cook over a low heat until thickened. Chill.

2. Prepare vanilla cream: beat egg yolks and sugar in a large bowl until light and fluffy.
Put milk, cream and vanilla pod into a saucepan and bring to just below boiling point. Remove vanilla pod and scrape black seeds into milk. Pour hot milk mixture into yolks, stir and return to pan. Cook on low heat without boiling for 10-15 minutes, or until slightly thickened. Chill thoroughly.

3. Sandwich every 2 meringues with a teaspoon of lemon cream.

4. To serve: pour some of the vanilla cream into the bottom of individual bowls, add a few meringue "sandwiches", and serve.

BAKED APPLES WITH VANILLA CUSTARD AND SOFT MERINGUE

mele coperte alla meringa

INGREDIENTS:

2 lbs. cooking apples
1½ oz. butter
Juice of 1 lemon
1 tablespoon sugar

CUSTARD:

6 egg yolks
1 cup castor sugar
3 tablespoons cornstarch
3 cups milk
Peel of 1 lemon, cut in a single long
    strip, if possible
1 vanilla pod, sliced open
    lengthwise

MERINGUE:

6 egg whites
½ cup castor sugar

1. Peel and halve apples, core, and cut into ¼ inch thick slices.

2. Melt butter in a large frying pan, add apples and stew for 5-6 minutes. Add lemon juice and sugar, stir and cook for 2 minutes. Arrange the apple slices in a single layer in an oval ovenproof dish.

She selects the apples with great care perhaps for a tart, or maybe for "mele coperte alla merii   "

3. Prepare the custard: beat egg yolks and sugar until pale and fluffy, sift in cornstarch and fold until evenly blended.

4. Put milk, lemon peel and vanilla pod in a small saucepan and bring to just below boiling point. Remove vanilla pod and scrape black seeds into milk. Discard pod. Remove and discard lemon peel.

5. Stir milk into egg yolks and cook over a low flame until mixture simmers and thickens. Remove from heat.

6. Beat egg whites and sugar until stiff.

7. Preheat oven to very low (275° F., 150° C.). Pour vanilla custard over the apples and cover with a layer of the beaten egg whites. Bake for 30-40 minutes. Serve either hot or cold.

PEACH TART

INGREDIENTS:

DOUGH:

2 cups flour
4 oz. butter
1 egg
$\frac{1}{3}$ cup castor sugar
A pinch of salt
2-3 tablespoons water

FILLING:

2 large, ripe peaches
3 eggs
$\frac{1}{2}$ cup castor sugar
$\frac{3}{4}$ cup cream
Grated rind of 1 lemon
4 large, firm, ripe peaches
3 tablespoons apricot jam
3 tablespoons brandy

1. Prepare the dough: put all ingredients in a food-processor fitted with a plastic blade, and work to a smooth dough. Add more water if dough is too dry. Gather up into a ball, wrap in a plastic bag and chill for at least 1 hour.

2. Roll out dough to a circle $\frac{1}{4}$ inch thick, and line a pie dish. Cut off excess dough and prick bottom with a fork. Preheat oven to medium (350° F., 180° C.).

3. Prepare the filling: peel peaches, stone and chop finely. Put eggs, sugar, cream, grated lemon rind, and chopped peaches in a bowl and beat well. Pour filling into pastry shell and bake for 40-50 minutes. Remove and chill.

4. Peel the 4 peaches, halve, stone, and slice thinly. Arrange in concentric circles over filling.

5. Put jam and brandy in a small saucepan, heat for 3-4 minutes and brush peaches.

The peach tart was photographed in the Piazza del Campo in Siena two days before the Palio – the traditional annual race, held for centuries.

FIG TART

INGREDIENTS:

DOUGH:

2 cups flour
1 teaspoon baking powder
4 oz. butter
4 tablespoons castor sugar
1 egg
A little ice water

FILLING:

4 egg yolks
3/4 cup castor sugar
2 tablespoons cornstarch
1 cup milk
1/2 cup cream
Rind of 1 lemon, peeled in a single
    strip if possible
About 20 ripe figs
4 tablespoons apricot jam
4 tablespoons brandy

1. Prepare the dough: put all ingredients in a food-processor fitted with a plastic blade, and work to a smooth dough. If dough is too dry, add more water. Gather into a ball, wrap in a plastic bag and chill for at least 1 hour.

2. Prepare the custard: beat egg yolks and sugar in a large bowl until pale and fluffy, sift in cornstarch and fold until evenly blended. Put milk, cream and lemon peel into a small saucepan and bring to a boil. Remove and discard lemon peel. Pour mixture over beaten yolks and return to saucepan. Cook over a low heat, stirring constantly with a wooden spoon, until thickened. Allow to cool.

3. Wash figs and quarter lengthwise.

4. Preheat oven to medium (350° F., 180° C.). Roll out dough to a circle 1/4 inch thick, and line a decorative pie dish. Prick bottom with a fork. Place greaseproof paper over the dough and fill with dried beans. Bake for about 15 minutes. Remove paper and beans and bake a further 20 minutes. Allow to cool.

5. Pour custard into baked shell and chill.

6. Arrange fig quarters in concentric circles (placing them cut side down and peel side down, alternately, as in picture).

7. Heat jam and brandy for 3-4 minutes in a small saucepan. Brush figs with jam glaze, and chill.

CUSTARD FILLED YEAST CAKE IN STRAWBERRY SAUCE

INGREDIENTS:

½ quantity of yeast dough for "Rich Raisin Cake" (p. 214) (omit raisins and candied orange peel)

CUSTARD:

4 egg yolks
¾ cup castor sugar
3 tablespoons cornstarch
1 cup milk
½ cup cream
1 vanilla pod, sliced open lengthwise

SAUCE:

1 lb. strawberries or raspberries
Juice of ½ lemon
½ cup castor sugar
1 tablespoon brandy

1. Preheat oven to medium-high (400° F., 200° C.). Shape dough into an elongated loaf 4 inches long and 2 inches high. Bake for about 40 minutes, allow to cool and store in refrigerator.

2. Prepare the custard: beat egg yolks and sugar until pale and fluffy. Gently sift in cornstarch. Put milk, cream and vanilla pod into a saucepan and bring to a boil. Remove pod, scrape black seeds into milk, and discard pod. Pour hot milk mixture over yolks, return to the saucepan and cook on a low heat, stirring all the time, until

mixture thickens. Make sure the custard does not boil. Chill thoroughly.

3. Prepare the sauce: Put strawberries or raspberries in a food-processor fitted with a steel blade and work to a smooth puree. Add lemon juice, sugar and brandy, stir, and chill.

4. Slice baked dough in two. Using a spoon, carefully scoop out some of the soft contents, to make a hollow. Fill with vanilla custard and store in refrigerator.

5. Divide sauce among flat serving plates. Cut filled cake into 1 inch thick slices, place a slice in the center of each plate, garnish with sliced fruit and serve.

CREAM FILLED CREPES

INGREDIENTS:

PRALINE POWDER:

1/2 cup hazelnuts
1/2 cup sugar

THE CREPES:

1 1/2 cups plain flour
3 tablespoons sugar
A pinch of salt
4 eggs
2 cups milk
1 1/2 oz. butter, melted
1 oz. butter (for frying)

FILLING:

1 cup cream
1 tablespoon castor sugar
1 teaspoon vanilla
1 quantity vanilla cream (p. 194)

1. Prepare praline powder: put nuts and sugar in a small saucepan and cook over a low heat, stirring occasionally, until sugar dissolves and caramelizes. Pour mixture onto a lightly oiled metal tray and allow to cool. When cool, break up caramelized nuts into a food-processor fitted with a steel blade and grind to a coarse powder.

2. Prepare the crepes: put flour, sugar, salt and eggs in a bowl and beat well. Gradually stir in milk. Add melted butter and stir until no traces of flour remain.

3. Melt a little butter in a no-stick frying pan, pour in a tablespoon or more of the batter and shake so that it covers the bottom of pan in a even layer. Cook about 2 minutes, turn and cook one more minute.

4. Whip cream with sugar and vanilla essence until stiff.

5. Fill crepes with whipped cream and fold.

6. To serve, pour a little vanilla cream on flat plates, place two crepes on each plate and sprinkle with praline powder.

CHEESE AND PINE NUT TART

INGREDIENTS:

DOUGH:

2 cups flour
4 oz. butter
1 egg
4 tablespoons sugar

FILLING:

3 eggs
³/₄ cup castor sugar
1 lb. fresh ricotta
1¹/₂ oz. softened butter
Grated rind of 1 lemon
3 oz. pine nuts
1 tablespoon butter
4 tablespoons apricot jam
4 tablespoons brandy

1. Prepare the dough: put all ingredients in a food-processor fitted with a plastic blade, and work to a smooth dough. Add 3 tablespoons cold water if necessary. Gather dough into a ball, wrap in a plastic bag and chill for at least 1 hour.

2. Preheat oven to medium (350° F., 180° C.). Roll out dough to a circle ¹/₄ of an inch thick, and line a decorative pie dish. Cut off excess dough and prick bottom with a fork.

3. Prepare the filling: Beat eggs with sugar. Add ricotta, butter, grated lemon rind and half of the pine nuts. Pour filling into pastry case and bake in preheated oven for about 45 minutes. Chill.

4. Fry remaining pine nuts in a tablespoon of butter until lightly browned. Sprinkle on tart.

5. Heat jam and brandy in a small saucepan for about 3 minutes and carefully brush tart with the mixture. Chill.

The pine-nuts give this cheese-tart its unique flavor.

STUFFED DRIED FIGS

INGREDIENTS:

30 dried figs
¼ cup rum or brandy
½ cup honey
1 teaspoon fennel seeds
30 blanched almonds

1. Make a small slit at the side of each fig, so it can be slightly opened. Sprinkle a little rum inside slit.

2. Put honey, fennel seeds and almonds in a bowl and mix well.

3. Insert an almond, a little honey, and some fennel seeds into every fig. Allow to stand for an hour and serve.

PRATO ALMOND BISCUITS

biscotti di prato

INGREDIENTS:

7 oz. shelled almonds
5 oz. unroasted peanuts
1 lb. flour
1 level teaspoon baking powder
1 lb. castor sugar
4 eggs
1 teaspoon vanilla
1 tablespoon grated orange rind
A pinch of salt
A little butter

1. Preheat oven to medium high (400° F., 200° C.). Roast almonds and peanuts for a few minutes, remove, and chop very coarsely.

2. Put the flour in a large bowl, add baking powder, eggs, sugar, vanilla, orange rind, and salt. Knead until soft and elastic (if too dry, add a little water), add roasted almonds and peanuts, and knead for a few more minutes.

3. Shape dough into thin elongated loaves, 2 inches wide and 1-1½ inches high. Put on a greased and floured baking sheet. Reduce oven temperature to medium (350° F., 180° C.) and bake for about 15 minutes.

4. Remove from oven, allow to cool for a few minutes, cut diagonally into ½ inch thick slices and return to oven. Bake 20-25 more minutes, or until lightly browned. The resulting hard biscuits are served with glasses of sweet wine (vermouth, port, Marsala), into which they are dunked.

SIENESE SPICE CAKE

panforte di siena

INGREDIENTS:

7 oz. shelled almonds
7 oz. shelled hazelnuts
1/4 teaspoon ground coriander
1/4 teaspoon ground cloves
1/2 teaspoon grated nutmeg
3/4 teaspoon cinnamon
10 oz. chopped candied fruit
3 oz. chopped dried figs
3 tablespoons cocoa powder
1 1/2 oz. flour
3 oz. honey
5 oz. castor sugar
Icing sugar

1. Preheat oven to medium-high (400° F., 200° C.). Roast almonds and nuts for a few minutes, remove and chop very coarsely.

2. Put almonds and nuts in a large bowl, add spices, candied fruit, figs and cocoa powder. Sift in flour and mix well.

3. Put honey and sugar in the top of a double boiler and cook, stirring all the time, until sugar dissolves and the mixture is slightly thickened.

4. Pour honey mixture over nuts and mix until evenly distributed.

5. Line a baking dish with greaseproof paper brushed with melted butter. Shape mixture into a rounded loaf 1-1 1/2 inches high, and place on baking sheet. Reduce oven temperature to medium (350° F., 180° C.) and bake for about 40 minutes. Sprinkle with icing sugar and serve.

RICH ALMOND BISCUITS

ricciarelli

INGREDIENTS:

11 oz. shelled almonds
1 cup castor sugar
1 tablespoon grated orange rind
2 egg whites
1 cup castor sugar

1. Grind almonds in the food-processor as finely as possible, and place in a bowl. Add sugar and grated orange rind and mix well.

2. Beat egg whites until stiff, then fold in sugar.

3. Fold ground almonds into egg whites until evenly distributed.

4. Line a baking sheet with greaseproof paper and brush with a little butter. Using a spoon, shape dough into biscuits 2 inches long and 1/2 an inch high and space evenly on baking sheet. Allow to rest for an hour.

5. Preheat oven to very low (250° F., 140° C.), and bake the little cakes for 15-20 minutes. Remove, allow to cool slightly and sprinkle with a little icing sugar.

The "panforte di Siena" and the "biscotti di Prato"; in the background, a view of Siena from the town hall.

EASTER CAKE

INGREDIENTS:

DOUGH:

3 oz. butter
1/2 cup sugar
2 egg yolks
2 cups flour
1 teaspoon baking powder

FILLING:

1 lb. fresh ricotta
3/4 cup sugar
Ground cinnamon
Juice of 1 lemon
Grated rind of 1 lemon
3 oz. chopped candied orange peel
5 eggs, separated
2 cups milk
3 oz. rice
1 1/2 oz. pine nuts

1. Prepare the dough: put all ingredients in a food-processor fitted with a plastic blade, and work to a smooth dough. Cover with a plastic sheet and chill for at least 1 hour.

2. Put ricotta, sugar, cinnamon, lemon juice, grated lemon rind and candied orange peel in a bowl and mix well.

3. Add the 5 yolks, one at a time, stirring well after each addition.

4. Put rice and milk in a saucepan, bring to a boil, reduce heat and cook, stirring occasionally, until all the milk has been absorbed. Allow to cool and fold into the cheese mixture.

5. Beat egg whites until stiff and fold into cheese mixture. Add pine nuts and fold.

6. Roll out two thirds of the dough into a 1/4 inch thick circle, and use to line a 10 inch round baking tin. Press dough into bottom and sides of tin and prick all over with a fork. Roll out remaining dough and cut into long, 1 inch wide strips.

7. Fill pastry case with the cheese mixture, and arrange dough strips over filling in a lattice pattern. Press strips to edges of case.

8. Preheat oven to medium (350° F., 180° C.). Bake the cake for about 50 minutes. Remove from oven. Before serving, sprinkle with a little icing sugar.

VARIATION: Add 3 tablespoons of cocoa powder to the filling.

RICH RAISIN CAKE

INGREDIENTS:

1 cup lukewarm milk
3/4 cup sugar
1 oz. fresh yeast
1 1/2 lbs. flour
3 eggs
8 oz. butter, softened
1 teaspoon salt
3 oz. raisins
2 tablespoons finely chopped candied orange peel

GLAZE (OPTIONAL):

2 egg yolks
8-10 tablespoons icing sugar
A little lemon juice

1. Pour milk in a large bowl, add yeast and sugar and stir until dissolved. Add one cup of the flour and stir. Cover with a damp towel and allow to rise in a warm place for about an hour.

2. Add eggs, butter, sugar and salt, then gradually stir in the remaining flour.

3. Transfer dough to a floured work surface and knead. Add raisins and grated orange rind and knead until smooth and elastic. Allow to rise in a warm place for about an hour, then knead again for half a minute.

4. Preheat oven to medium-high (400° F., 200° C.). Shape dough into a loaf (rounded, elongated, or a plait). Put on a greased baking sheet, brush with beaten egg yolk and bake for about 50 minutes.

5. For the glaze, beat the yolks with 4 tablespoons of the icing sugar and a little lemon juice. Gradually add 4-6 tablespoons icing sugar, beating all the time. Pour over baked cake and allow to dry.

Even the most patriotic Italian vintners will admit that no Italian wines can be found among the half dozen great wines of the world. Not yet, some will add. But when it comes to a way of life, wine drinking with its merriment, obtaining the best wine, most suitable to the food on the table, the mood round the table, and the state of your pocket – Italy is truly a foretaste of paradise.

Nowhere in the world will you find such a delightful variety of wines. Simple and young homemade wines, found in all manner of village pubs: light wines, some slightly fermented, like the Lombroscci coming from the Parma region, served chilled with the famous Parmesan, at ridiculous prices; the heavy red Southern wines, which nearly evaporate on the way from your glass to your lips on a hot day, accompanying the heavy food which is always seasoned with tomato juice, garlic, and olive oil, and strangely seem to warm not only the body but the heart and soul as well, and leave the pink sweat stain on the shirt – the mark of a good meal.

Tuscany: vineyards covering the hills of this beautiful region, which produces vast quantities of wine. Starting at the commercial chianti, emerging from the factory in a straw wrapped bottle, wine which tourists relate, above all other wines, to Italy, and is responsible above all others for its bad reputation; all the way through to the brunello, the most noble of Italian wines, ageing for years in the Montalcino cellars; and in the middle of this wonderful range of wines, and the amazingly reasonable price range accompanying it, a young light chianti, sold in grocery stores out of a giant glass bottle – you come with your bottle, and the vendor moves a couple of quarts into your bottle with a hose – cheaper than Coke. A thick layer of olive oil floats at the top, sealing air out of the wine, to keep it from going sour; classico, from the very heart of the chianti region, wine with much more body and personality; chianti classico riserva, for which the very best chianti grapes are selected. The wine is aged in casks and then, after no less than five years in the bottle, it is a wonderful accompaniment to the Bistecca Fiorentina, the luscious steak made in this region.

Sparkling Wines: Northern Asti, a small village on the road to Turin, which is also renowned for its marvellous cuisine, manufactures vast amounts of Asti's Spumante. This is not a noble wine, like the French champagne, nor as expensive, but when it is dry, it is a lovely opening for a meal, and when sweet, an excellent dessert wine. A very fresh wine, naturally fermented, except that its fermentation is done in giant stainless-steel containers, not in the bottle, as in the case of champagne. This fermentation lasts three to six months, not years, like champagne, and the price is in the table wine range, again unlike champagne.

In Asti the "Methode Champenoise" is manufactured, according to the traditional French champagne method, with huge cellars and row upon row of diagonally laid bottles, and vintners passing by each and turning half turns, and three year ageing and all ceremony pertaining to it. But this is more of 'we can too'. In the best case the Asti "Methode Champenoise" is as good as French champagne, but it is generally not so good. Asti's strength lies in the simpler spumante, which brings this noble drink back down to earth, and makes it possible to enjoy it in a simple, inexpensive meal, the kind of meal which can only be so wonderful in Italy.

A little way south, round the town of Elba, some of Italy's best wine is made. Above all others is the barolo – a rich wine, full bodied, ages well. This and a six to ten year Bruli can accompany any meal. and goes marvelously with strong cheese, or the brunello, which has been discovered by the world only recently, and whose prices rose rapidly ever since. A good brullo may still be obtained at a reasonable price, while brulli and barbasco are less noble wines from the same area – less expensive, and drunk younger.

Italy is a land of red wines. One can go south to the Puglia expanses, where more wine is manufactured than anywhere else in Italy, or climb north, drink the local cheap red wine, and not miss even once. Things are more complicated when it comes to white wine. Here the simple local wine will indeed be a simple wine. Anyone who ate wonderful fresh seafood and washed it down with local white wine – knows the taste of disappointment. One hundred and fifty kilometers north of Rome – and we still haven't found any wine worth writing home about. For those who are meticulous about their white wines, we would recommend a trip much farther north, to the regions bordering on Austria or Switzerland. The Pinot Grirgir, is a grape from which very pleasurable dry wines are manufactured in Northern Italy – wines which are quite a good bet; Gavi, from north western Piemonte is an excellent bet, very dry with a fruity bouquet and a shade of adventure, one of those which stings the palate and favors it as well.

The Chardonnay wines, made of a grape which has only recently become widely popular in Italy, are simply a gamble – we drank some good Chardonnays, some mediocre, and quite a few bad ones.

But perhaps the most important thing to stress in the Italian wine lists are the prices: even in the best and most expensive restaurants, the best wines are sold at a few dozen dollars a bottle, rather than a few hundred, as in France. You will not have to mortgage your home in order to learn a great deal about Italian wines, and discover whether you prefer the full bodied Barolo to the light Chianti Classico, and whether it is worth your while to spring for the difference and go for a Barolo.